IDENTIFYING TREES

An All-Season Guide
to Eastern North America

0 11557 03360 1

IDENTIFYING TREES

An All-Season Guide to Eastern North America

Michael D. Williams

STACKPOLE
BOOKS

Published by
STACKPOLE BOOKS
5067 Ritter Rd.
Mechanicsburg, PA 17055
www.stackpolebooks.com

Printed in China

10 9 8 7 6 5 4 3 2 1

First edition

Cover design by Caroline Stover
Cover photos by Michael D. Williams

Library of Congress Cataloging-in-Publication Data

Williams, Michael D., forester.
    Identifying trees : an all-season guide to Eastern North America / Michael D. Williams. — 1st ed.
        p. cm.
    Includes index.
    ISBN-13: 978-0-8117-3360-1
    ISBN-10: 0-8117-3360-2
    1. Trees—East (U.S.)—Identification. 2. Leaves—East (U.S.)—Identification.
    I. Title.

QK477.2.I4W55 2007
582.160974—dc22

                                                                        2006010857

Contents

The goal of this book is to make tree identification fun and easy—even in the winter. It covers most of the trees found growing in eastern North America. My wish is for this work to help you learn the given names and appreciate the wonders of the trees around you. Enjoy!

Acknowledgments

This volume represents the fruits of many years of professional forest management experience. During this time, countless writers, fellow foresters, ecologists, and woodsmen shared their tricks and skills in tree identification. It also builds upon the foundation laid by the authors who went before me.

Several people helped make this book possible. Nathan Waters patiently taught me how to use a digital camera. Gerald Shelton freely shared his lifetime of mountain wisdom. David Smith and Mark Stanley introduced me to the trees in the bottomlands and swamps of the low country. Each used keen observation to help locate various hard-to-find trees and made sure they were properly identified and collected.

Thanks to Dr. Scott E. Sclarbaum, Professor, Department of Forestry, Wildlife and Fisheries at the University of Tennessee; Dr. Dale Thomas, retired Professor and past Director of Herbarium at Northeast Louisiana University; and Tom Simpson, Regional Urban Forester for the Tennessee Division of Forestry, who reviewed this book and gave much-needed, productive advice that helped improve it. Special thanks to Tom for serving as technical advisor during the final editing. A special thank you to Mrs. Barbara Thomas and Larry Tankersley, who used their vast editing skills to turn my rough manuscript into a usable text. Finally, thanks to Mark Allison and Ken Krawchuk at Stackpole Books for their continued support of this project.

Almost a hundred years ago, Joyce Kilmer penned the famous line, "but only God can make a tree." All of us who live and work in and around the forests of the eastern United States know the joy of living surrounded by reminders of God's creative genius, and I am thankful for the wonderful creation that trees are.

PART ONE

Leaf Identification

Tree leaves all have characteristics that, when known, make identifying the tree that produced them possible. These general characteristics are described, and a leaf characteristic key is provided for use in matching a sample leaf or leaves to the correct name of the tree. Because the leaves of some trees can be quite variable in both size and shape, the leaf shape and size most often encountered on each tree is presented for reference. This is followed by detailed accounts of various tree species.

1

Kinds of Leaves

The first step in the identification process is asking yourself what kind of leaves you see. Are they needlelike, scalelike, or broad and flat?

NEEDLELIKE LEAVES

Needlelike leaves are long and slender. They get their name because they look like sewing needles. They may stand alone on the twig, grow in clusters, or be wrapped at the base in bundles of two to five needles each.

SCALELIKE LEAVES

Scalelike leaves are very small, overlapping one another like the scales of a fish. Juvenile scalelike leaves may stand erect and be prickly.

 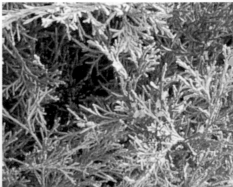

BROAD AND FLAT LEAVES

Broad and flat leaves are broad, flat, and thin. They have many shapes and sizes, but all are much wider and longer than thick.

Broad and flat leaves have several unique properties that can be compared in order to identify the tree that produced them.

Simple or Compound

Broad and flat leaves may be either simple or compound. **Simple leaves** have a single leaf blade and stalk, called a *petiole,* which is directly attached to the limb at the point called the *node.* **Compound leaves** have two or more leaf blades, often called *leaflets,* attached to a central leaf stalk, which in turn is attached to the twig at the leaf node, where a bud will also be found.

Simple leaf   *Compound leaf*

Opposite or Alternate

Broad and flat leaves may have either **opposite** or **alternate** arrangement along the twig. Simple or compound leaves attached directly across from one another at the same point (node) on the twig are said to have an **opposite** arrangement. Simple or compound leaves attached at offset, zigzag intervals, where the leaves are never straight across from one another along the stem, are said to have an **alternate** arrangement.

Opposite

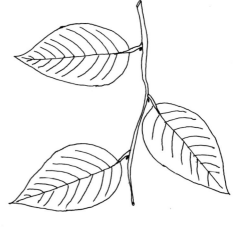

Alternate

Broad and Flat Leaf Parts

Broad and flat leaves have distinguishing characteristics that can be used to separate one from the other. To ease identification, these different characteristics have all been given names.

- The farthermost point of the leaf away from the twig is called the *leaftip,* or *apex.*
- The closest point of the wide, flat blade portion of the leaf joining the leaf stalk is called the *leaf base.*
- The *node* is the point where the leaf stalk attaches to the twig.
- The stalk between the base of the leaf and the leaf node is called the *petiole.*
- On compound leaves, the portion of the stalk between leaflets is called the *rachis.*
- The large, flat, green portion of the leaf is called the *blade.*
- On compound leaves, the blades are often called *leaflets.*
- Leaf blades, veins, and stalks may be *pubescent*, or have hairs growing from their surfaces.

Simple Leaf Parts

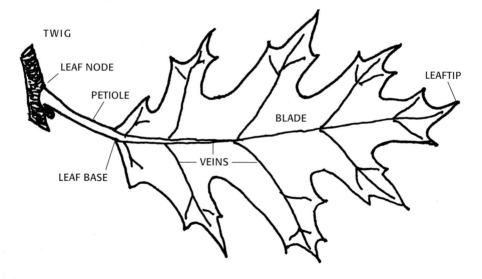

TWIG

LEAF NODE

PETIOLE

LEAFTIP

BLADE

VEINS

LEAF BASE

Compound Leaf Parts

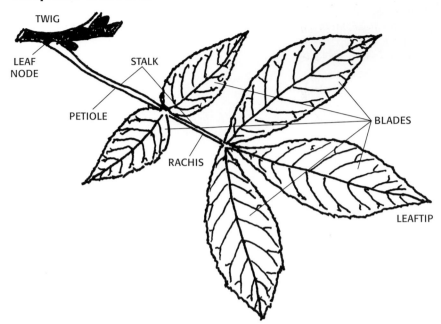

Leaf Margins

The edge of the broad and flat leaf or leaflet is called its *margin*. The margin may be either smooth or toothed. Teeth may be fine, coarse, or both on the same edge. They may also be blunt.

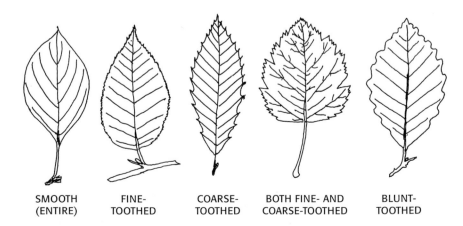

SMOOTH (ENTIRE) FINE-TOOTHED COARSE-TOOTHED BOTH FINE- AND COARSE-TOOTHED BLUNT-TOOTHED

Broad and flat leaf margins may have dips, called *sinuses,* and bulges, called *lobes.* If the margins are continuous and unbroken, with no indentations, they are called *entire.*

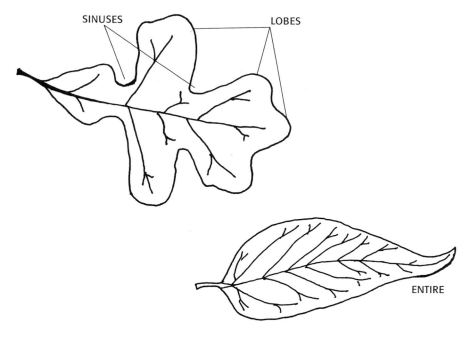

SINUSES   LOBES

ENTIRE

Lobes and sinuses come in many different shapes that can be used to identify trees. The lobes may have either rounded or pointed ends, or they may have spiked ends, toothed edges, or both at the same time. The sinuses may be either rounded or V-shaped.

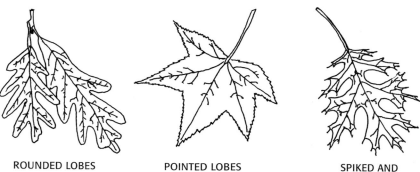

ROUNDED LOBES
AND SINUSES

POINTED LOBES

SPIKED AND
TOOTHED LOBES

USEFUL ID TIPS

- Expect variability. Leaves may vary in size on the same tree. Those growing in the shade or on sprouts are often much larger than those exposed to full sun.
- Sometimes more than one leaf shape grows on the same tree.
- Almost all flat-bladed leaves are a lemon-lime color in the spring, become darker shades of green as the summer progresses, and take on various bright colors in the fall. Leaf pictures in this book are from all seasons.
- Learn bark characteristics and tree shapes as quickly as possible, as leaves are not present on many trees at least half of the year.
- Tree bark is oldest, thickest, and roughest at the base of the trunk and youngest, thinnest, and smoothest on the branch tips. There is usually a slow transition in bark pattern and thickness between the two points.
- The usual bark characteristics may be absent from some trees. When this is the case, look for other identifying characteristics.
- Use all of your senses. Some trees may have a unique smell, taste, or feel that helps in identification.
- If necessary, supplemental identification clues can be gathered from the leaves, twigs, and fruit lying on the ground under the tree. Keep in mind, however, that these items may have come from a neighboring tree.
- To identify trees not listed in this book, collect or photograph samples that include a stem with several leaves and buds, and then go to the Internet or other ID books to make the identification. Typing "tree identification" in your search engine will usually locate several good sites.
- Relax and have fun. Even professional foresters occasionally have trouble identifying trees.

Vein Patterns

Broad and flat leaves have different vein patterns that can be used to help with identification. Leaves may have a central vein running from base to point or notch, with secondary veins branching out at various points along the central vein, or they may have several major veins that spread up from a central point at base of the leaf.

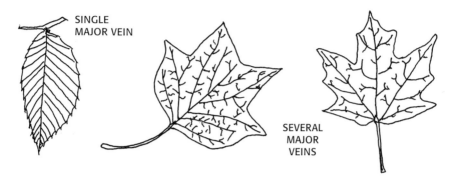

SINGLE
MAJOR VEIN

SEVERAL
MAJOR
VEINS

POISON IVY, SUMAC, AND OAK ALERT

Poison Ivy and Poison Sumac are two plants in the eastern United States that should be avoided because of the itchy rash that often occurs after contact with them. Poison Oak is native to the western United States, but its name recognition is so great that it is also included in this text. Each of these three plants produces a toxic oil-based sap called urushiol, which sticks to the skin and may cause the rash. Contact with almost any part of these plants any time of year can cause the skin to break out. Avoidance is the best protection. Many people

Virginia Creeper is often confused with Poison Oak.

Poison Ivy

Poison Sumac

have reported good results taking an oral ivy extract that builds immunity. The sap can be washed off with soap and water up to thirty minutes after exposure. After that time, there are many commercial products that can be used with varying results. The three plants are described and pictured here to help you avoid them. A plant that grows in the East and is often misidentified as Poison Oak is Virginia Creeper, a harmless common vine that sometimes climbs forest trees. Its compound leaves have five leaflets, clustered on each twig end.

Poison Ivy is a common deciduous forest vine, losing its leaves during the winter. It grows along the ground and often climbs trees. When it climbs a tree, it sometimes becomes so large and thick that it can be mistaken for part of the tree to which it is attached. Climbing Poison Ivy vines are dark brown, very hairy, and closely attached to the supporting tree. The many closely spaced branches of the vine may reach out 3 feet (.9 m) or more from the tree. The vine may climb 1⅔ feet (.5 m) or more up the tree. Poison Ivy leaves have three stalked leaflets clustered at the branch tips. Leaflets average 3 to 5 inches (76.2 to 127 mm) long and 2 to 4 inches (50.8 to 101.6 mm) wide. They may be entire, have a sharp-pointed, tooth-shaped lobe on one side, or have one tooth-shaped lobe on each side. This vine can be found growing in a wide variety of conditions, from swamps to mountains. It is very common throughout most of the eastern United States.

Poison Sumac is a bush or small tree that commonly grows in pure thickets in many of the wet areas in the East. The leaves grow alternately along the stem. This is useful in distinguishing them from the ashes, whose leaves are opposite one another. The leaves are deciduous, falling off in winter, compound, and 7 to 12 inches long (177.8 to 304.8 mm), with seven to thirteen boat-shaped leaflets that are each 2 to 4 inches (50.8 to 101.6 mm) in length and 1 to 2 inches (25.4 to 50.8 mm) in width. The leaflets are smooth, shiny dark green above and pale below, with smooth edges. When present, the ripe berries are waxy white.

Poison Oak

Poison Oak is a small tree, bush, or climbing vine that is native to the western United States and most commonly found west of the Rocky Mountains. The leaves usually have three (sometimes more) leaflets, typically growing in sets, with the terminal leaflet at the end of a long stalk and the side leaflets attached at the base of the stalk, without secondary leaf stalks. Leaflets have variable shapes but generally resemble small oak leaves, with rounded lobes and sharp V-notched sinuses. When broken, the twig will ooze a white sap.

2

Leaf Identification Key

The following key uses the described characteristics needlelike, scalelike, and broad and flat leaves to identify the tree the leaf came from. It does so by asking questions about the sample leaf's unique characteristics and referring the reader to new questions based on the answer.

Each question closes in on the identity of the tree by eliminating all the tree leaves that do not match the answer. In the end, the key provides a photograph and illustration of the leaf that matches the sample and gives the name of the tree it came from. Usually the tree can be identified in fewer than five steps. Page numbers following the common trees refer to the species account.

A. If your sample leaves are needlelike or scalelike, go to number *1* on page 13.

B. If your sample leaves are broad and flat, go to number *2* on page 27.

1. NEEDLELIKE OR SCALELIKE LEAVES

a. If your sample leaves are scalelike, go to *Scalelike Leaves* below.
b. If your sample leaves are single and needlelike, go to *Single Needles* on page 15.
c. If your sample leaves have two to five needles wrapped in each bundle, with a sheath at the base of the leaf needles, go to *Bundled Needles* on page 21.

Scalelike Leaves

Compare your sample with the following trees:

Atlantic White-cedar	*Northern White-cedar*
Eastern Redcedar	*Southern Redcedar*

ATLANTIC WHITE-CEDAR page 386

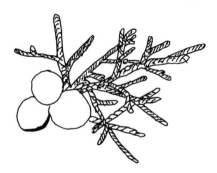 

Very small, prickly, scalelike, blue-green leaves grow on four sides of randomly pointing twigs. Branches are very thin and grow from tree at right angles. Tree is usually found growing in bogs and wet areas. Rounded fruit are ½ to ¾ inch (12.7 to 19.1 mm) in diameter and hangs from a peg. Open fruit look like clusters of thick, rounded shields held together at a center point.

EASTERN REDCEDAR   page 234

Juvenile growth forms small, needlelike leaves that later develop into very small, blue-green, scalelike, prickly leaves growing on all sides of the limb to form a thick, tight, aromatic, prickly top. When present, the fruit are very small, light gray berries. Small branches turn sharply upward.

NORTHERN WHITE-CEDAR   page 388

Very smooth, dark, evergreen, small scalelike leaves growing on four sides of the center twig, forming a pattern similar to that of a herringbone bracelet or necklace. Scale-covered twigs begin with a single stem and then spread out in flat, fan-shaped sprays of foliage. The fruit are small, erect, ½-inch (12.7 mm)-long cones, standing on short stems, that open into six to twelve scales, staying on the tree for a year before falling off. These cones resemble tiny pinecones.

SOUTHERN REDCEDAR page 236

Dark green, tiny, evergreen scales grow opposite one another in four diamond-shaped rows that form long, smooth, slender, four-angled twigs standing out independent of one another, with open space between twigs. Tree may have a single stem, or if the top has been lost or damaged, it may have two or more spreading trunks that sometimes curve out at a long, sweeping, upward angle. This tree is usually found growing in sand along the eastern and southern coastline.

Single Needles

Compare your sample with the following trees:

Baldcypress	*White Fir*	*Norway Spruce*
Pondcypress	*Carolina Hemlock*	*Red Spruce*
Balsam Fir	*Eastern Hemlock*	*White Spruce*
Fraser Fir	*Blue Spruce*	*Tamarack*

BALDCYPRESS page 152

Needles have sharp tips and are ½ to ¾ inch (12.7 to 19.1 mm) long, lime green to yellow-green, growing featherlike in two rows along lateral branches. Needles turn yellow then dull red and drop off in fall.

PONDCYPRESS page 350

Lime green ¼-inch (6.4 mm) needles are loosely woven around thin, soft center twigs that gently curve out from the main branch like sea grass waving in ocean currents. Needles turn yellow, then reddish brown and drop off in the fall.

BALSAM FIR and **FRASER FIR** page 198

 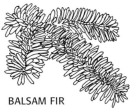 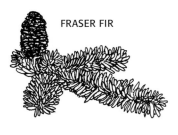

FRASER FIR

BALSAM FIR

Evergreen leaves are needlelike, about 1 inch (25.4 mm) long, with blunt or sometimes notched points and slightly tapered bases that are attached directly to the stem in a spiral arrangement. The bottom of each needle has two parallel, bluish white stripes along the entire lower length that make the needles look silver-gray from below. The leaves on the bottom of the stem turn upward, leaving the illusion of a rounded, green tail that is flattened along the bottom. Cut ends of cross-sectioned leaves have long, oval shape.

Balsam Fir and Fraser Fir are nearly identical within the leaves. Only the cones and the evidence of resin pockets in the bark can be used to distinguish the two, and only then with caution.

FRASER FIR

WHITE FIR

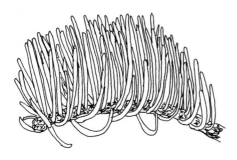 

Light blue-gray colored, upward-curving needles are 2 to 3 inches (50.8 to 76.2 mm) long, growing in a scattered fashion that makes them look as if they only are growing on the upper three sides of the twig. Needles are flattened on the top and bottom. White Fir is native to the West and is only occasionally found in urban areas as an ornamental. Originally an introduced species.

CAROLINA HEMLOCK page 206

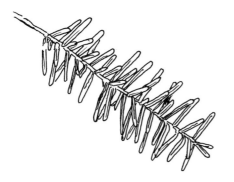 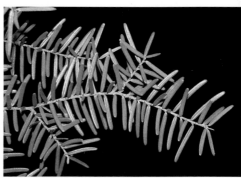

Flat, evergreen needles are ½ to 1 inch (12.7 to 25.4 mm) long with blunt ends. They usually have two light blue lines parallel along the length of the bottom of each leaf. Scattered needles stick out from stem in all directions.

EASTERN HEMLOCK   page 208

 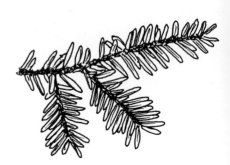

    Flat, evergreen needles are ½ to ¾ inch (12.7 to 19.1 mm) long with blunt ends. Two light blue lines run parallel along the length of the bottom of each leaf. Needles lie compactly flat along the branches, with some needles sticking up.

BLUE SPRUCE   page 366

    Sharp-pointed, stiff, curved evergreen needles are decidedly light blue-green to steel gray–blue in color and are ¾ to 1¼ inches (19.1 to 31.8 mm) long, with needles coming off all sides of a stout, yellow branch.

NORWAY SPRUCE page 368

Stiff, sharp-pointed, dull green, evergreen, four-sided, sharp-pointed needles are ½ to 1 inch (12.7 to 25.4 mm) long, standing on very short posts. Needles grow from all sides of the branch in gentle curves toward the branch tip. Secondary branches tend to droop down, while the main branches curve upward. When present, cones 4 to 6 inches (101.6 to 152.4 mm) long hang from the tips of the branches. Introduced species used in residential plantings.

RED SPRUCE page 370

Crowded, bright yellow-green, evergreen needles are ⅜ to ⅝ inch (9.5 to 15.9 mm) long, four-sided, sharp-pointed, and square when cross-sectioned and looked at from cut end. Needles grow out from all sides of the twig on short, woody pegs. Often crosses with black spruce to form hybrids.

WHITE SPRUCE page 372

Bluish green needles with white lines on the bottom are ½ to ¾ inch (12.7 to 19.1 mm) long and clustered around all sides of the branch, growing from short pegs. Four-sided evergreen needles have a pungent odor when crushed.

TAMARACK

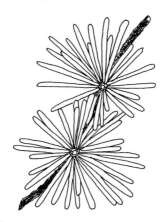

Light blue-green needles are ¾ to 1 inch (19.1 to 25.4 mm) long, three-angled, very soft, and slender, clustered in rosettes on spur twigs. Needles may also grow as singles toward branch tip. Twigs are stout and orange-brown in color. Needles turn yellow in fall and drop for the winter. Cones stand erect on top of the branch, are ½ to ¾ inch (12.7 to 19.1 mm) tall, and persist throughout the winter. An extreme northern tree, Tamarack is found only as far south as northern New Jersey but is abundant in Canada.

Bundled Needles

Compare your sample with the following trees:

Austrian Pine	*Longleaf Pine*	*Shortleaf Pine*
Eastern White Pine	*Pitch Pine*	*Slash Pine*
Jack Pine	*Red Pine*	*Table Mountain Pine*
Loblolly Pine	*Scotch Pine*	*Virginia Pine*

AUSTRIAN PINE page 328

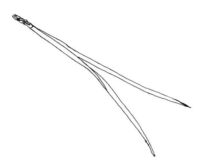

Needlelike, evergreen leaves are 3 ½ to 6 inches (88.9 to 152.4 mm) long and bundled in sets of two. They are slender, stiff, often shiny, and dark blue-green in color. Limbs grow from tree in whorled sets.

EASTERN WHITE PINE page 330

Evergreen needles are packaged five per bundle. They are soft, flexible, blue-green and 3 to 5 inches (76.2 to 127 mm) long. Each needle has white lines along the length of the bottom side. The bark is dark gray-black with silver touches. The limbs grow from the trunk at distinct intervals in whorls.

JACK PINE page 332

Stiff, stout, evergreen, sometimes twisted, dark green to grayish green needles, 1½ to 2 inches (38.1 to 50.8 mm) long, packaged in bundles of two needles each. Needles fork away from one another. The tree is generally a ragged-looking, small pine tree growing on poor soils in the northeastern states and Canada.

LOBLOLLY PINE page 334

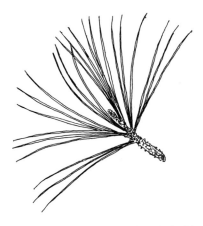

Evergreen needles growing in bundles of three. The bundle sheath is ½ inch (12.7 mm) or longer. Needles 6 to 9 inches (152.4 to 228.6 mm) long, yellow-green to gray-green and slender but stiff. The needles often form round ball-shaped tufts around end of branch, giving the illusion of the branch holding the ball straight out at its center point.

LONGLEAF PINE page 336

Very long, dark green, slender, flexible, evergreen needles are 10 to 16 inches (254 to 406.4 mm) long and bundled in groups of three. Needles are tufted toward the ends of the branches, where they hang down. A large, silver-scaled bud is located at the end of each branch.

PITCH PINE page 338

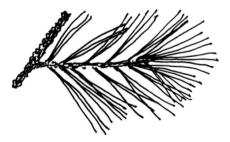 

Evergreen needles growing in bundles of three (sometimes two). Needles are often twisted and 3 to 5 inches (76.2 to 127 mm) long. Often there are needles growing directly out of trunk as well as from the branches.

RED PINE page 340

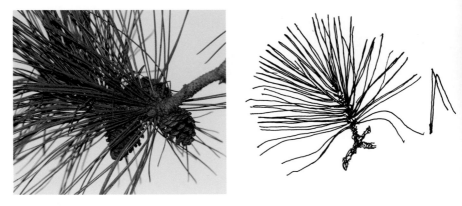

Slender, flexible, evergreen needles, 4 to 6 inches (101.6 to 152.4 mm) long, break easily when bent double; grow in bundles of two, whose branches grow opposite one another in whorls. Tree trunk is usually limb-free and has long, wide, reddish brown bark plates. Most often found growing in the northern states and Canada.

SCOTCH PINE

Stiff, evergreen needles growing in bundles of two. Blue-green, twisted, slightly flattened, and flaring needles from 1 to 4 inches (25.4 to 101.6 mm) long, with many lines of stomata visible. Needle tips are sharp. Light brown twigs. Introduced tree usually found in urban settings or windbreaks and cultivated mainly for Christmas trees. A native of Europe and Asia, it has been naturalized in the northern United States especially in New England.

SHORTLEAF PINE page 342

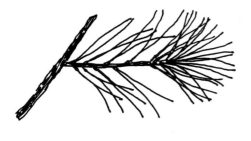

Evergreen needles growing with two (sometimes three) in each bundle. Slender, flexible needles 2 ¼ to 4 ½ inches (57.2 to 114.3 mm) long grow in clumps that turn upward, giving the illusion from a distance of needle tufts sitting on top of the branches. Small, round resin pockets are often present on bark plates.

SLASH PINE page 344

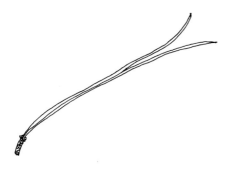

Evergreen needles are stiff, dark green, 6 to 10 inches (152.4 to 254 mm) long, with two (sometimes three) needles per bundle, held by a basal sheath that is usually less than ½ inch (12.7 mm) long. The drooping needles are clustered toward the ends of bare, orange-brown, stout branches, often looking like primitive brooms. When present, pinecones grow from branch at an angle turned back toward the central trunk. Usually found growing along the coastal plains of the Deep South.

TABLE MOUNTAIN PINE page 346

Evergreen needles 1½ to 3 inches (38.1 to 76.2 mm) long, growing in bundles of two each. Needles are dark green, thick and stiff, and sometimes twisting. The tree has dark brown, rough bark and fat cones with a heavy spike at the end of each spiraled scale bract. Tree is usually found growing above 2,500 feet (762.2 m) in elevation.

VIRGINIA PINE page 348

Evergreen needles 1½ to 3 inches (38.1 to 76.2 mm) long growing in bundles of two each, with the needles usually spreading out in a V-shape from each other. Needles are stiff, dull green in summer and yellow-green in winter, twisted and spreading. When present, the cones are small and reddish brown. Tree bark is thin and scaly, with retained dead limb stubs. The foliage appears thin and lacy when looking up through foliage.

2. BROAD AND FLAT LEAVES

a. If your sample leaves are very large and fan-shaped, compound, and growing in long sets of palm fans, go to *Fan-shaped Leaves* on page 28.

b. If your leaves have an opposite arrangement and are simple, go to *Opposite Simple Leaves* on page 28.

c. If your leaves have an opposite arrangement and are compound, go to *Opposite Compound Leaves* on page 35.

d. If your leaves have an alternate arrangement and are simple, go to *Alternate Simple Leaves* on page 43.

e. If your leaves have an alternate arrangement and are compound, go to *Alternate Compound Leaves* on page 94.

Fan-shaped Leaves

Compare your sample with the following tree:

Sabal Palmetto

SABAL PALMETTO page 322

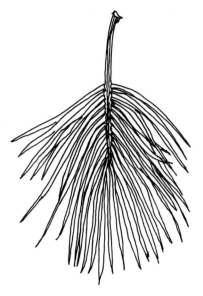

Huge, evergreen, fan-shaped, compound leaves, 4 to 7 feet (1.2 to 2.1 m) long, with opposite rows of sword-shaped leaflets growing along opposite sides of a long central stalk that is flat on top and rounded on the bottom. Leaves all hang from cluster at top of tree and droop down sides, giving the classic look of the palmetto palm tree.

Opposite Simple Leaves

Compare your sample with the following trees:

Northern Catalpa	*Drummond Red*	*Silver Maple*
Southern Catalpa	*Maple*	*Striped Maple*
Flowering Dogwood	*Mountain Maple*	*Sugar Maple*
Black Maple	*Norway Maple*	*Southern Sugar*
Chalk Maple	*Red Maple*	*Maple*

NORTHERN CATALPA page 174

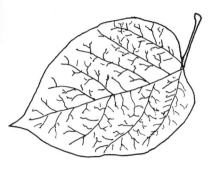

Opposite or three-leaf (whorled) pattern with simple, heart-shaped leaves 6 to 12 inches (152.4 to 304.8 mm) long and 4 to 8 inches (101.6 to 203.2 mm) wide, thin-textured, smooth above, furry below, and odorless when crushed. Twiglike seedpods are 9 to 20 inches (228.6 to 508 mm) long, blunt-tipped, and are filled with seeds that are 1 inch (25.4 mm) long, square-tipped, and winged.

SOUTHERN CATALPA page 176

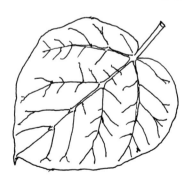

Opposite or three-leaf (whorled) pattern with simple, heart-shaped leaves 5 to 10 inches (127 to 254 mm) long and 4 to 7 inches (101.6 to 177.8 mm) wide, rather thick-textured, smooth on top and downy on the bottom. When the leaf is crushed, it gives off a foul odor. Slender seedpod is sticklike, 9 to 20 inches (228.6 to 508 mm) long, very sharp-tipped, and contains many sharp-tipped, winged seeds.

FLOWERING DOGWOOD page 186

 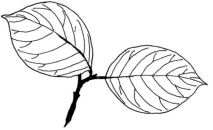

Opposite, simple leaves are football-shaped, 3 to 5 inches (76.2 to 127 mm) long, and 2 to 3 inches (50.8 to 76.2 mm) wide, with smooth but wavy outer edges. The veins make pronounced upward-sweeping curves from the centerline of the leaf to the smooth outside edge.

BLACK MAPLE page 258

 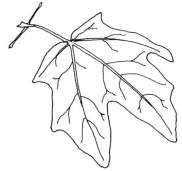

Opposite, simple leaves with three (sometimes five) lobes. Leaves are 4 to 5 ½ inches (101.6 to 139.7 mm) long and wide, with rounded sinuses and long lobes that end in narrow, blunted tips. Leaves have a tendency to droop and look wilted. The upper blade surface is smooth and dark green; the lower surface is lighter-colored and covered with fine fuzz. The leaf stalk, or petiole, is long and fuzzy. There is often one or sometimes two opposite, long, narrow, spurlike growths called stipules protruding from the petiole's base just before the junction with the twig.

CHALK MAPLE

Opposite leaves are 2 to 3 ½ inches (50.8 to 88.9 mm) long, with three (occasionally five) blunt, often drooping, lobes. Both lobes and sinuses are rounded. Smooth margins are wavy. The upper leaf surface is smooth; the lower surface is hairy. Seeds have widely spread wings. Chalk Maple is a rare tree that is often found only as an ornamental in the South.

DRUMMOND RED MAPLE

Opposite, simple leaves are 2 ½ to 4 inches (63.5 to 101.6 mm) in length and width, with wide, pointed, toothed lobes. Usually there are three large lobes and sometimes two smaller ones. The sinuses between lobes form sharp V-notches. The top of the leaf is smooth; the bottom surface is white with fine, downy hairs. Hair also grows on the new-growth twigs. This rare tree is a variety of Red Maple and is only found in the deep swamps of the Mississippi Valley.

MOUNTAIN MAPLE

Opposite leaves are three-lobed (sometimes slightly five-lobed), 3 to 5 inches (76.2 to 127 mm) long and almost as wide, with an irregular shape. Yellowish green top; paler bottom covered with fine gray fuzz. Margins are coarsely toothed. Usually an understory shrub or small tree. Native from northeastern Canada to New England with pockets found along the Appalachian Mountains as far south as northern Georgia.

NORWAY MAPLE

Opposite leaves are 4 to 7 inches (101.6 to 177.8 mm) long, and usually a little wider than long. They are five-lobed (slightly sometimes seven-lobed) and have five main veins radiating out from the central stalk at the notched base of the leaf blade. Shallow lobes are smooth-edged with occasional long teeth. The leaf blade is dull green above, with sunken veins. It is smooth below except for occasional tufts of hairs in vein angles. The leaf stalk, or petiole, is long and produces white sap when broken. Norway Maple is widely planted as an ornamental but is native to Europe.

RED MAPLE page 262

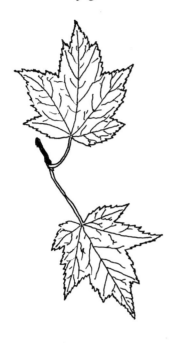

Opposite, simple leaves are 2 ½ to 4 inches (63.5 to 101.6 mm) in length and width, with wide, pointed, toothed lobes. Usually there are three large lobes and sometimes two smaller ones. The sinuses between lobes form sharp V-notches. Leaf edges are sawtoothed.

SILVER MAPLE page 264

Opposite leaves are 6 to 8 inches (152.4 to 203.2 mm) long, with prominent, pointed, coarse-toothed lobes and narrow, rounded sinuses. Bottom of leaf is silvery color.

STRIPED MAPLE page 266

Opposite leaves are three-lobed above center, finely toothed, 4 to 6 inches (101.6 to 152.4 mm) long and almost as wide. Lobes are short, wide, and pointed. Leaf is lime green above and pale below, smooth on both sides. Young tree trunk is usually light green with light blue stripes. Larger trees have brown bark and are striped only along branches.

SUGAR MAPLE page 268

Opposite, smooth leaves are 3 to 5 inches (76.2 to 127 mm) long and wide. The edges are smooth except for a few long, pointed teeth. There are five main lobes that have pointed tips. Deep U-shaped sinuses between lobes. Petiole and top surface of leaf blade are smooth. The veins along the lower surface are hairy. There are five main veins radiating out from the base of the leaf blade. The leaf stalk does not produce white sap when broken.

SOUTHERN SUGAR MAPLE

Opposite, simple leaves are 4 inches (101.6 mm) long by 3 inches (76.2 mm) wide, with three large forward-pointing lobes and occasionally two smaller lobes or coarse teeth toward the base. Sinuses are U-shaped; edges are smooth. The leaf blade is smooth on top and covered with fine, velvetlike hair underneath. Southern Sugar Maple is considered by many to be a southern variety of Sugar Maple which it often hybridizes with.

Opposite Compound Leaves

Compare your sample with the following trees:

Biltmore Ash	*Pumpkin Ash*	*Painted Buckeye*
Black Ash	*Red Ash*	*Red Buckeye*
Blue Ash	*White Ash*	*Yellow Buckeye*
Carolina Ash	*Boxelder*	*Horsechestnut*
Green Ash	*Ohio Buckeye*	*Paperbark Maple*

BILTMORE ASH

Opposite, blue-green, compound leaves, 8 to 12 inches (203.2 to 304.8 mm) long, have five to nine (usually seven) leaflets growing along the sides and end of the leaf stem. The bottom of each leaflet blade and twig ends are covered with fine, white hair. Twig ends look large and blunt. Buds are halfway to completely covered by the leaf stalk's junction to the stem. The tree has a limited range (southern Appalachian) and is almost indistinguishable from White Ash.

BLACK ASH page 138

Opposite, compound leaves, 10 to 17 inches (254 to 431.8 mm) long, with seven to eleven (usually nine) finely sawtoothed leaflets 3 to 5 inches (76.2 to 127 mm) long attached in pairs (except at the end) to central stalk, with *no leaflet stalk.*

BLUE ASH page 140

Opposite, compound leaves, 8 to 12 inches (203.2 to 304.8 mm) long, with seven to eleven leaflets that are 3 to 5 inches (76.2 to 127 mm) long and 1 to 2 inches (25.4 to 50.8 mm) wide. Each leaflet is rounded at the base, pointed at the tip, and finely toothed along the margin, with a dark yellow-green upper surface and a lighter-colored lower surface. Both surfaces are smooth. The twigs holding the leaves are four-angled, with four almost flat sides, and may also have a small wing at each corner.

CAROLINA ASH

Opposite, compound leaves are 4 to 10 inches (101.6 to 254 mm) long, with five or seven thick, leathery leaflets. Dark green, shiny leaflets are 1 to 4 inches (25.4 to 101.6 mm) long and ¾ to 2 inches (19.1 to 50.8 mm) wide and have finely toothed edges. Carolina Ash is a small swamp species of limited range and no economic importance.

GREEN ASH page 142

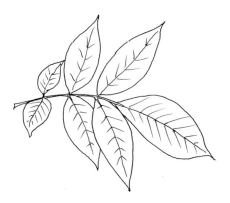

Opposite, blue-green, compound leaves, 8 to 12 inches (203.2 to 304.8 mm) long, have three to seven leaflets, 2 to 5 inches (50.8 to 127 mm) long, growing along the sides and end of the leaf stem. Twig ends look large and blunt. A prominent bud can be seen nestled in the crotch between the twig and leaf petiole.

PUMPKIN ASH

Opposite, compound leaves are 10 to 18 inches (254 to 457.2 mm) long, with seven (sometimes nine) long, spear-shaped leaflets that have tapered bases and pointed tips. Small bud is almost buried in the crotch between the branch and leaf petiole. Leaflets are 4 to 9 inches (101.6 to 228.6 mm) long and 1 ½ to 3 inches (38.1 to 76.2 mm) wide, with smooth to slightly toothed edges. Northern leaves usually have woolly lower surfaces and stalks, whereas southern leaves and stalks may be smooth. The tree is only distinguishable from Red Ash by the leaves and fruit. This introduced tree is generally common only in deep swamps and flooded river bottoms in the South and Midwest.

RED ASH   page 144

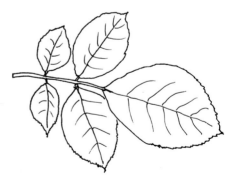

Opposite, blue-green, compound leaves, 8 to 12 inches (203.2 to 304.8 mm) long have three to seven leaflets, 2 to 5 inches (50.8 to 127 mm) long, growing along the sides and end of the leaf stem. Leaflet bottom surfaces and twig ends are covered with dense, white hair. Twig ends look large and blunt. A prominent bud can be seen partially nestled in the crotch between the twig and leaf stem node.

WHITE ASH page 146

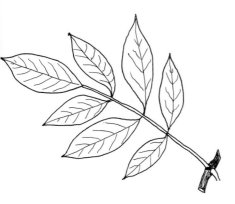 

Opposite, blue-green, compound leaves, 8 to 12 inches (203.2 to 304.8 mm) long, have five to nine (usually seven) leaflets growing along the sides and end of the leaf stem. Twig ends look large and blunt. Little or no bud is visible at the leaf stalk junction.

BOXELDER page 168

Opposite, compound leaves 5 to 15 inches (127 to 381 mm) long. The 3 to 5 leaflets are 2 to 4 inches (50.8 to 101.6 mm) long and have several lobe shapes, with some jutting out to the side like pointed thumbs. Edges are coarsely toothed. Twigs are long, slender, and often green.

OHIO BUCKEYE

Opposite, compound leaves, with five leaflets spreading out in a fan shape from a central point at the end of the leaf stem. Leaflets are dark green above and yellowish green below, usually 4 to 6 inches (101.6 to 152.4 mm) long, with broad, pointed tips and tapered bases. Margins may have both fine and coarse teeth. Leaves give off foul odor when crushed. Fruit pod is spiked. Predominatley a midwestern tree, Ohio Buckeye has the largest range of the buckeye family.

PAINTED BUCKEYE

Opposite, compound leaves with five leaflets spreading out in a fan shape from a central point at the end of the leaf stem, which is 8 to 12 inches (203.2 to 304.8 mm) long. Leaflets are dark green above and lighter below. Usually a shrub, but may be small tree. Reproduces from runners forming clumps. Grows in cool, damp upland areas. Painted Buckeye is a shrub or small tree and is common only in the southern piedmont.

RED BUCKEYE

Opposite, compound leaves usually have five (rarely seven) leaflets fanning out from a central point like blades on a fan. The leaf stalk, or petiole, is 4 to 6 inches (101.6 to 152.4 mm) long; the dark green blades are 4 to 6 inches (101.6 to 152.4 mm) long and 1½ to 2½ inches (38.1 to 63.5 mm) wide, with sharp, double-toothed edges. Usually found as a cluster of shrubs or a small tree in damp to wet lowland areas. Primarily a southern tree, it is widely planted as an ornamental because of its red flowers.

YELLOW BUCKEYE page 170

Opposite, compound leaves, with five leaflets spreading out in a fan shape from a central point at the end of the leaf stem. Leaflets are dark green above and yellowish green below, usually 4 to 6 inches (101.6 to 152.4 mm) long, with broad, pointed tips and tapered bases. Margins may have both fine and coarse teeth. No smell is present when crushed. Skin of fruit husk is smooth.

HORSECHESTNUT   page 232

Opposite, compound leaves with seven leaflets that are 4 to 10 inches (101.6 to 254 mm) long and 2 to 5 inches (50.8 to 127 mm) wide, spreading out in a fan shape from a central point at the end of the leaf stem. Leaflets are dark green on both top and bottom. Large buds are very shiny and sticky. Skin of fruit husk is spiny or warty.

PAPERBARK MAPLE   page 260

Opposite, compound leaves each made up of three blue-green leaflets that are 3 to 6 inches (76.2 to 152.4 mm) long by 2 to 2 ½ inches (50.8 to 63.5 mm) wide, attached at a central point on the stalk. Leaflet edges are coarsely toothed to lobed. The leaflet base and petiole are covered with a thick mat of white hair. Bark is thin and peels from the side.

Alternate Simple Leaves

1. If your leaves do not have lobes, go to *Simple Entire Leaves* on page 44.

2. If your leaves have rounded lobes, go to *Simple Rounded Lobes* on page 80.

3. If your leaves have pointed lobes, go to *Simple Pointed Lobes* on page 86.

SIMPLE ENTIRE LEAVES

a. If your leaves do not have teeth along the edges, go to *Smooth Edges* on page 45.

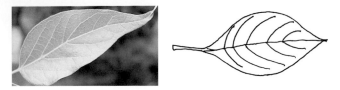

b. If your leaves have fine teeth along the edges, go to *Fine-toothed Edges* on page 57.

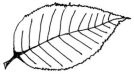

c. If your leaves have coarse teeth along the edges, go to *Coarse-toothed Edges* on page 66.

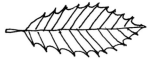

d. If your leaves have both fine- and coarse-toothed edges, go to *Both Fine- and Coarse-toothed Edges* on page 71.

e. If your leaves have blunt teeth along the edges, go to *Blunt-toothed Edges* on page 77.

Smooth Edges
Compare your sample with the following trees:

Smoketree	Southern Magnolia	Osage-orange
Carolina Cherry-laurel	Sweetbay Magnolia	Paulownia
	Umbrella Magnolia	Pawpaw
Alternate-leaf Dogwood	Laurel Oak	Persimmon
	Southern Live Oak	Redbud
Sugarberry	Oglethorp Oak	Black Tupelo
Bigleaf Magnolia	Shingle Oak	Swamp Tupelo
Cucumber Magnolia	Willow Oak	Water Tupelo
Fraser Magnolia		

SMOKETREE page 362

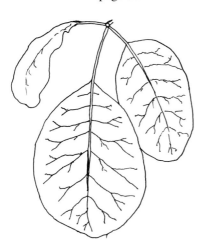 

Alternate, egg-shaped leaves are 2 to 6 inches (50.8 to 152.4 mm) long and 1 ½ to 3 inches (38.1 to 76.2 mm) wide, with dull green upper surface and a lighter lower surface that is covered with hairs when young, becoming smooth later in the summer. Crushed leaves give off a distinctive mint odor.

CAROLINA CHERRYLAUREL   page 180

Alternate, simple leaves are 2 to 4 ½ inches (50.8 to 114.3 mm) long and ¾ to 1½ inches (19.1 to 38.1 mm) wide, oval-shaped and pointed at both ends, evergreen, with an orange to red petiole and thick leaf blades that are glossy dark green on top and pale green beneath. Edges are usually smooth but may have an occasional tooth. Leaf gives off a pleasant cherry scent when crushed.

ALTERNATE-LEAF DOGWOOD

Alternate, broad leaves with V-shaped bases and tips and rounded midsections are 3 to 5 inches (76.2 to 127 mm) long and 2 ½ to 3 ½ inches (63.5 to 88.9 mm) wide. Veins are prominent, sweeping gracefully from the center vein to the outside leaf edge in curves that match the curve of the leaf edge. Leaves are alternate but often clustered at branch tips. A small tree or shrub, it is cultivated as an ornamental for its brilliant yellow or red fall color and its showy flowers. Alternate-leaf Dogwood is found in rich, moist soil of forests or near streams.

SUGARBERRY page 204

Alternate, simple, light green leaves are 2 to 4 inches (50.8 to 101.6 mm) long and 1 to 2 inches (25.4 to 50.8 mm) wide. Mostly smooth-edged, though there may be an occasional tooth. Lopsided base, arrowhead-shaped body, and long slender tip. Three major veins originate from the leaf petiole and then flare out up through the leaf.

BIGLEAF MAGNOLIA page 246

Alternate, very large, thin leaves are 20 to 30 inches (508 to 762 mm) long and up to 12 inches (304.8 mm) wide. Lower leaf surface is white. Leaves flare out from prominently eared bases to widest point over halfway to a bluntly rounded tip. Twigs are stout, yellow-green, and furry. Terminal buds are 1½ to 2 inches (38.1 to 50.8 mm) long and covered with white woolly hairs.

CUCUMBER MAGNOLIA page 248

Alternate, large, dark green leaves (lighter beneath) are 6 to 10 inches (152.4 to 254 mm) long and broadly spear-shaped, with rounded bases and tapered tips. Bottom of leaf is covered with soft, fine hairs. Thick petiole is short. Leaves grow in scattered fashion along the stem.

FRASER MAGNOLIA page 250

 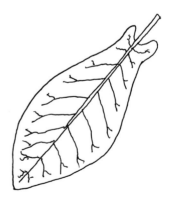

Alternate, large, thin, spear-shaped, simple leaves, 8 to 18 inches (203.2 to 457.2 mm) long, with eared base and broadly pointed tip. Lustrous, bright green top and smooth, pale green bottom. Blade edges are smooth. Terminal buds are large and purple-green.

SOUTHERN MAGNOLIA page 252

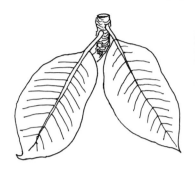 

Alternate, evergreen leaves 5 to 8 inches (127 to 203.2 mm) long and 2 to 3 inches (50.8 to 76.2 mm) wide. They are smooth, thick, and leathery, with a glossy green upper surface and pale with rust-colored hairs below. The edges are entire, cupping slightly downward. The petiole is thick and has rusty-colored hairs along its stem.

SWEETBAY MAGNOLIA page 254

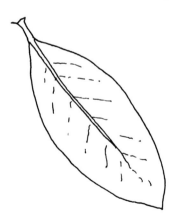 

Alternate, canoe-shaped, tough, leathery leaves, 3 to 5 inches (76.2 to 127 mm) long and 1 to 1½ inches (25.4 to 38.1 mm) wide, clustering toward the branch tip. Top surface is lustrous yellow-green; bottom surface and petiole are covered with fine, white hairs. A crushed leaf smells spicy.

UMBRELLA MAGNOLIA page 256

Alternate, broad, spear-shaped leaves are 10 to 24 inches (254 to 609.6 mm) long and 5 to 10 inches (127 to 254 mm) wide, spreading out from the branch like the spokes of an umbrella from the clustered points of origin. Each leaf has a pointed base and pointed tip. Large terminal buds are smooth and purplish green.

LAUREL OAK page 280

 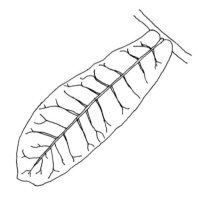

Alternate, leathery-textured, smooth-edged, and bristle-tipped leaves are 2 to 4 inches (50.8 to 101.6 mm) long and ½ to 1 inch (12.7 to 25.4 mm) wide. They are clustered toward the ends of the branches. The shape is very narrow at the short petiole, gently flaring out to the widest area past midpoint and then rounding down to the tip. Upper surface of the leaf blade is dark green and smooth; leaf is smooth and lighter colored beneath. Leaves are semievergreen, holding onto the tree until new foliage comes out in the spring. Unlike other oaks, twigs will break easily when bent.

SOUTHERN LIVE OAK page 312

Alternate, simple leaves are 2 to 5 inches (50.8 to 127 mm) long and ½ to 2 inches (12.7 to 50.8 mm) wide. They are thick, leathery, and stiff, with pointed bases and rounded tips. The top leaf surface is dark green; the bottom is pale and usually downy. Leaf edges often curl downward. Trees have long, twisted branches. Leaves are evergreen, although they often fall in the spring after the new leaves have appeared.

OGLETHORP OAK

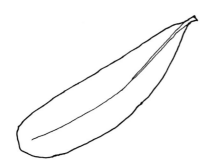

Alternate, boat-shaped leaves with blunt tips are 2 to 5 inches (50.8 to 127 mm) long and ¾ to 1½ inches (19.1 to 38.1 mm) wide. They are bright green on top and lighter green on the bottom. The bottom surface is covered with star-shaped clusters of yellow hairs. Leaf edges are smooth but sometimes wavy. Tree is large, with a straight trunk and twisted branches. This tree has a very limited range, found growing only in mid–South Carolina and mid-Georgia.

SHINGLE OAK page 288

Alternate, leathery-textured leaves are 4 to 6 inches (101.6 to 152.4 mm) long and 1 to 2 inches (25.4 to 50.8 mm) wide. Leaf has a rounded base, parallel sides, and rounded end tapering to a small bristle tip. Blade is smooth and glossy on top, lighter beneath. Fine white hairs cover the bottom surface. Edges are entire. Petiole is short and fuzzy.

WILLOW OAK page 300

 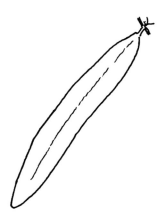

Alternate, thick, long, narrow, smooth leaves are 2 to 5 inches (50.8 to 127 mm) long and ½ to 1 inch (12.7 to 25.4 mm) wide, with spiked tips. Leaf blade has a light green top surface; beneath it is pale and often covered with fine, gray hairs.

OSAGE-ORANGE page 320

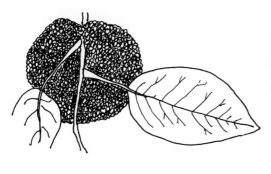

Alternate, simple leaves are shaped like wide-bodied boats, with wedge-shaped bases, pointed tips, and entire edges. They are 3 to 5 inches (76.2 to 127 mm) wide and 2 to 3 inches (50.8 to 76.2 mm) wide, with slender petioles that are 1 to 1½ inches (25.4 to 38.1 mm) long. Both the dark green upper surface and pale green lower surface are smooth. Fruits look like green, rough-textured oranges and can reach the size of softballs. Puncturing the fruit will result in a white, milky juice oozing out, which soon turns black.

PAULOWNIA page 324

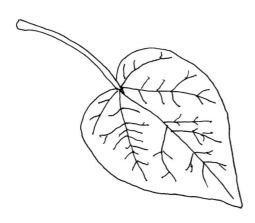

Alternate, large, broad, thin, heart-shaped leaves with entire edges (sometimes slightly three-lobed) are 5 to 12 inches (127 to 304.8 mm) long and almost that wide. The leaf blade is lightly hairy above and very hairy beneath.

PAWPAW

Alternate leaves are 7 to 10 inches (177.8 to 254 mm) long and taper gently from the base to the widest point about two-thirds of the way to the end, then round down to a pointed tip. The leaf edges are smooth. The top of the leaf is medium green, with prominent veins; the bottom is pale green. Buds are velvet brown. Broken or crushed twigs and leaves release a foul odor. It is a shrub or sometimes small tree that grows in deep, rich, and moist soils along streams and in bottoms. Pawpaw is commonly found as an understory plant under hardwood stands. It is principally known for its fruit which tastes like bananas.

PERSIMMON   page 326

Alternate, simple leaves are 4 to 6 inches (101.6 to 152.4 mm) long. They are oval with rounded bases and pointed tips, smooth edges, shiny dark green tops, and paler green bottoms. The petiole is ⅓ to 1 inch (8.5 to 25.4 mm) long and covered with tiny hairs. Trunk has dark, rough, knobby bark.

REDBUD page 354

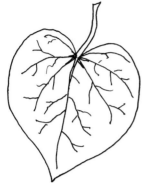

Alternate, heart-shaped leaves are 2 to 6 inches (50.8 to 152.4 mm) long and almost as broad, with a smooth top and bottom. Edges are smooth, and the tip is rather abrupt. The blade top is purple in spring, slowly turning dark green throughout summer and rusty red in fall; the bottom is pale green.

BLACK TUPELO page 378

Alternate, smooth-edged leaves are 2 to 5 inches (50.8 to 127 mm) long and have an oval spear-tip shape. Shiny dark green in color. Small, sharp tip often crooks to one side or curls downward. Leaves look as if they are attached to twigs in spiral pattern when seen from below. Tree grows in dry soils. Looking at the leaves from the branch end can give the illusion of a large daddy longlegs spider that is walking away.

SWAMP TUPELO   page 380

Alternate leaves, 1 ½ to 4 inches (38.1 to 101.6 mm) long and ½ to 1 ½ inches (12.7 to 38.1 mm) wide, have narrow, rounded bases and broad tips, with sides that reach their widest beyond the halfway point. Broadly rounded end tapers to a small tip. Upper blade surface is glossy green; lower surface is lighter and more or less covered by hairs. Tree is found growing in permanent standing water.

WATER TUPELO   page 382

Alternate leaves, 4 to 6 inches (101.6 to 152.4 mm) long and 2 to 4 inches (50.8 to 101.6 mm) wide, have narrow, rounded bases and broad tips, with sides that reach their widest beyond the halfway point. Broadly rounded end tapers to a small tip. Blade edges are usually smooth but occasionally may have one or more tapered teeth. Upper blade surface is glossy green; lower surface is lighter and more or less fuzzy. Tree is found growing in bottomlands that spend at least part of the year submerged in water. Often found growing at the edges of swamps and streams.

Fine-toothed Edges

Compare your sample with the following trees:

Common Alder	*Hackberry*	*Black Willow*
Quaking Aspen	*Downy Serviceberry*	*Coastal Plain*
Yellow Birch	*Smooth Serviceberry*	*Willow*
Carolina Buckthorn	*Carolina Silverbell*	*Pussy Willow*
Black Cherry	*Mountain Silverbell*	*Weeping Willow*
Fire Cherry	*Sourwood*	*White Willow*

COMMON ALDER

Alternate, football-shaped leaves are 2 ½ to 5 inches (63.5 to 127 mm) long and have fine-toothed edges. Both top and bottom leaf surface are smooth, but lower veins are usually hairy. Shrub or occasionally a small tree growing along streams and in wet places.

QUAKING ASPEN page 150

 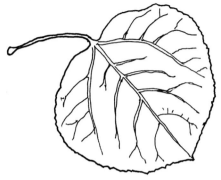

Alternate, simple, rounded leaves have short, abrupt tips and finely toothed margins. The thin but firm leaf blades are 1 to 2 inches (25.4 to 50.8 mm) long and wide, with lustrous, dark green upper surfaces and dull green lower surfaces. The petiole is thin and flattened, allowing the leaf to move in the slightest breeze. Greenish white bark is smooth with black markings.

YELLOW BIRCH page 166

 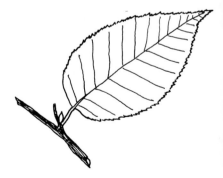

Alternate, simple leaves are 2 to 4 inches (50.8 to 101.6 mm) long. They often grow in slightly offset alternate pairs on short side twigs as well as in alternate singles. Leaf is arrowhead-shaped, with a rounded base and pointed tip. Dark, dull green above and yellowish green below, with finely toothed edges. Crushing the leaf or scratching the twig releases a mild wintergreen odor. Yellowish gray tree bark is thin and peels from the side in thin curls. Trunk has fine horizontal lines, or lenticels.

CAROLINA BUCKTHORN

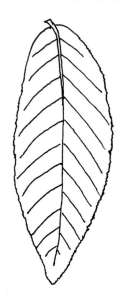

Alternate, simple leaves are finely toothed, 2 to 5 inches (50.8 to 127 mm) long, and prominently veined, with glossy, dark green top surfaces. Twigs give off a foul odor when broken or crushed. Usually a bush or small tree whose fruit reportedly has medicinal properties.

BLACK CHERRY page 178

Alternate, simple leaves are oval to spear-tip-shaped, 2 to 6 inches (50.8 to 152.4 mm) long, and 1 to 1½ inches (25.4 to 38.1 mm) wide. Many fine, incurved teeth break the edges. Leaf blade is thick and shiny dark green above, paler below with rusty-colored hairs along bottom leaf midvein. Small glands may protrude from either side of petiole just below leaf blade. Twig has pungent odor when scraped or broken.

FIRE CHERRY

Alternate, simple, arrow-point-shaped leaves with fine, sharp teeth along the margins are 3 to 4 inches (76.2 to 101.6 mm) long and approximately 1 inch (25.4 mm) wide. Shiny yellow green to dark green, and smooth on both top and bottom. Leaves are evenly spread up and down long, slender stems. Often called Pin Cherry. Fire Cherry is a small tree or shrub aptly named because it quickly generates itself after forest fires. Commonly found in Canada and Newfoundland, it is seldom found abundantly in the lower U.S., except in pockets of the southern Appalachians.

HACKBERRY page 202

Alternate, light green leaves, 2 to 4 inches (50.8 to 101.6 mm) long and 1 to 2 inches (25.4 to 50.8 mm) wide. Smooth-edged, lopsided base and arrow-head-shaped tip; finely toothed from base to tip. Three veins arise from tip of petiole. Tree trunk is light gray, with prominent corky warts in singles and clusters.

DOWNY SERVICEBERRY

Alternate leaves are 2 to 4 inches (50.8 to 101.6 mm) long and 1 to 2 inches (25.4 to 50.8 mm) wide. Arrowhead-shaped, with a rounded or heart-shaped base, pointed tip, and finely toothed edges. Petiole is very thin. Dark green above and pale to white below. Upper surface is smooth; lower surface begins hairy but ends the season smooth or with only a few silky hairs present. A large shrub or small tree, Downy Seviceberry has a large natural range and is commonly planted as an ornamental because of its showy clusters of white flowers.

SMOOTH SERVICEBERRY

Alternate leaves are 2 to 4 inches (50.8 to 101.6 mm) long and 1 to 2 inches (25.4 to 50.8 mm) wide. Arrowhead-shaped, with a rounded or heart-shaped base, pointed tip, and finely toothed edges. Petiole is very thin. Dark green above and pale to white below. Both surfaces are smooth. This small tree can grow quite large in the southern Appalachians and is native from Newfoundland to Georgia and west to Kansas. The sweet berries are favored by wildlife and used by some in pies and jellies.

CAROLINA SILVERBELL page 358

 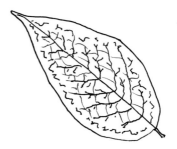

Alternate leaves are 3 to 5 inches (76.2 to 127 mm) long and spear-shaped, with a short leaf stalk. Rounded at the base, with a tapered tip and fine, sharp-toothed edges. Upper surface looks textured but is smooth to touch. Dark green above; pale lower surface may be slightly hairy. Small tree or large bush with maroon bark that cracks open in curvy, wide but shallow fissures, exposing various shades of tan inner bark.

MOUNTAIN SILVERBELL page 360

 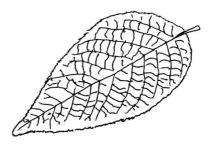

Alternate leaves are 8 to 11 inches (203.2 to 279.4 mm) long and spear-shaped. Rounded at the base, with a tapered tip and fine, sharp-toothed edges. Upper surface looks textured but is smooth and dark green; pale undersurface is slightly hairy. Trunk bark is dark maroon to blue-gray in color.

SOURWOOD page 364

Alternate, lance-shaped leaves are 4 to 7 inches (101.6 to 177.8 mm) long and 1 to 2 inches (25.4 to 50.8 mm) wide, with finely toothed margins. Hairs stick up along the bottom of the center vein when leaf is folded back in half along vein. The leaf has a deep green, smooth upper surface and a lighter surface below. Leaf has a very sour taste.

BLACK WILLOW page 390

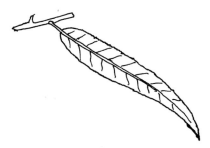 

Alternate, simple, thin leaves are bright green on both top and bottom, 4 to 6 inches (101.6 to 152.4 mm) long, and less than ½ inch (12.7 mm) wide. The leaf blade is rounded at the base, with a long, slender tip. Edges are finely toothed from base to tip, with tiny, yellow glands at or just under the tip of each tooth. Usually found in wet areas with full sunlight.

COASTAL PLAIN WILLOW

 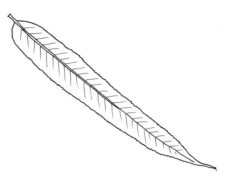

Alternate leaves are very long and slender, growing from 2 to 4 inches (50.8 to 101.6 mm) long and only ½ to ¾ inch (12.7 to 19.1 mm) wide. The leaf blade edge has fine, sawtooth-shaped teeth. The upper surface of the leaf is dark green, and the lower surface is white. The leaf is hairy in the spring, often becoming almost hairless by late summer. The leaf stalk, or petiole, is very hairy. Usually a shrub but sometimes grows into a small tree in the southeastern United States.

PUSSY WILLOW

 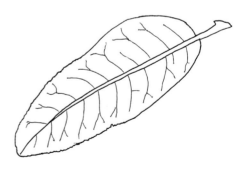

Alternate leaves are 1½ to 4 inches (38.1 to 101.6 mm) long and up to 1¼ inches (31.8 mm) wide. Edges have small, irregular teeth. The leaf is rounded at the base and rounds down to a point at the tip. The upper surface of the leaf is deep, lustrous green; the lower surface is white, with hair in the early spring and smoothing out by late summer. A many-stemmed shrub that may grow to be a small tree, it has been cultivated in the U.S. as an ornamental.

WEEPING WILLOW page 392

Alternate, slender leaves are 2½ to 5 inches (63.5 to 127 mm) long and only ¼ to ½ inch (6.4 to 12.7 mm) wide, with very fine, sharp teeth along edges. Leaves are dark green above and whitish or gray below. Branches are long, thin, and supple, often hanging straight down to the ground in lengths that may exceed 6 feet (1.8 m).

WHITE WILLOW page 394

Alternate, slender, deciduous leaves are 2 to 4½ inches (50.8 to114.3 mm) long and ⅜ to 1¼ inches (9.5 to 31.8 mm) wide, with fine, sharp teeth along the edges. The leaf blade is glossy green on top and silver-white below. The lower surface, and sometimes the upper, is covered with fine, silky hairs.

Coarse-toothed Edges
Compare your sample with the following trees:

Bigtooth Aspen	American Beech	Swamp Cottonwood
American Basswood	American Chestnut	American Holly
Mountain Basswood	Eastern Cottonwood	Sawtooth Oak

BIGTOOTH ASPEN page 148

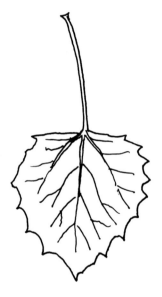

Alternate, rounded, arrowhead-shaped leaf blades are 2 ½ to 4 inches (63.5 to 101.6 mm) long, with large, irregular teeth. Leaf ends in a sharp tip. Petiole is flat on two sides. Bark is greenish white and smooth, with black markings.

AMERICAN BASSWOOD page 154

Alternate, heart-shaped leaves are 5 to 6 inches (127 to 152.4 mm) long, with one side of the base slightly higher than the other. Leaf blade is rounded to an abrupt tip, with coarse, sharp-toothed margins. Leaf is smooth on both top and bottom, with a slightly lighter shade of green on the bottom. Large trees usually have sprouts growing around the base.

MOUNTAIN BASSWOOD page 156

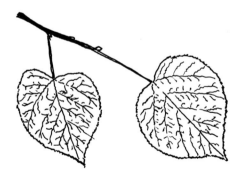

Alternate, heart-shaped leaves are 3 ½ to 5 inches (88.9 to 127 mm) long, with one side of the base much higher than the other. Leaf blade is rounded to an abrupt tip, with coarse, sharp-toothed margins. Bottom is pale greenish white. Large trees usually have sprouts growing around the base.

AMERICAN BEECH   page 158

Alternate, spear-shaped, sharp-tipped leaves are 3 to 5 inches (76.2 to 127 mm) long, with very prominent, straight veins that stand out along the underside, each ending in the center of a coarse tooth. Twig may have a pronounced zigzag pattern, with a long, slender bud and leaf at each outside turning point of the pattern.

AMERICAN CHESTNUT

Alternate, lance-shaped, pointed leaves are 5 to 8 inches (127 to 203.2 mm) long. Dull yellow-green top and smooth, lighter bottom. Evenly spaced, spine-tipped, coarse teeth give the appearance of a two-sided sawblade. Once a dominant forest tree, American Chestnut has been virtually eradicated by the chestnut blight. While the tree continues to regenerate as seedlings, it seldom obtains fruit bearing age before succumbing to the blight.

EASTERN COTTONWOOD page 184

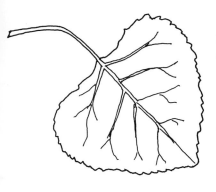

Alternate, triangular leaves are 3 to 5 inches (76.2 to 127 mm) long. Base is almost straight across. Medium coarse to rounded, toothed edges. Flexible, flat-sided petiole.

SWAMP COTTONWOOD

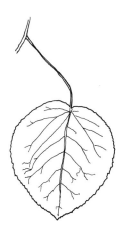

Alternate, wide, oval leaves dangling from a long, thin petiole. Leaf is 4 to 7 inches (101.6 to 177.8 mm) long and 3 to 6 inches (76.2 to 152.4 mm) wide. Base is round to slightly heart-shaped. Tip rounds down to a point. Edges have coarsely rounded teeth. Almost always found growing in or around swampy areas, Swamp Cottonwood has a limited range but has been planted as an ornamental.

AMERICAN HOLLY

    Alternate, thick, sharply spiked, toothed, evergreen leaves are 2 to 4 inches (50.8 to 101.6 mm) long, oval, and leathery. Lustrous dark green top and yellowish green bottom. Edges are often cupped downward. The foliage, branches, and fruit are often used for Christmas decorations. The tree is commonly planted as an evergreen ornamental.

SAWTOOTH OAK

    Alternate, simple, boat-shaped leaves are 4 to 7 inches (101.6 to 177.8 mm) long, with straight, parallel veins ending in noticeably long, evenly spaced, thin-spiked teeth. An introduced species from Asia, Sawtooth Oak is planted both as a shade tree and for wildlife.

Both Fine- and Coarse-toothed Edges

Compare your sample with the following trees:

Sweet Birch	*American Elm*	*Winged Elm*
Gray Birch	*Cedar Elm*	*Hophornbeam*
Paper Birch	*September Elm*	*Hornbeam*
River Birch	*Slippery Elm*	

SWEET BIRCH page 160

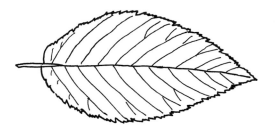

Alternate, irregularly double-toothed, elongated arrowhead-shaped leaves are 2 to 4 inches (50.8 to 101.6 mm) long. Dark green upper surface, turning light yellow in fall. Leaves are smooth both above and below except for fine hairs along the lower surface of the ten to thirteen vein pairs. Leaves and twigs give off a strong scent of wintergreen when scratched or crushed.

GRAY BIRCH

 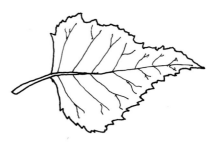

Alternate, simple, triangular leaves are 2 ½ to 3 inches (63.5 to 76.2 mm) long. Double-toothed edges with sharply pointed teeth. Smooth, shiny, dark green upper surface and paler bottom that often has orange blotches. Petiole is long, with glands at base. Tree bark is chalky white, with triangular dark lines below limbs, and does not peel. An introduced tree, Gray Birch is a short-lived tree also known as a pioneer tree because it rapidly grows in cleared areas of the northeast.

PAPER BIRCH   page 162

 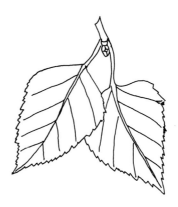

Alternate, triangular leaves are 2 to 4 inches (50.8 to 101.6 mm) long. Slightly rounded base and tip tapering to a point. Edges have both coarse and fine, sharp teeth. Leaf blade is dark green on top and lighter green on the bottom. Bark is white and peels from side.

RIVER BIRCH page 164

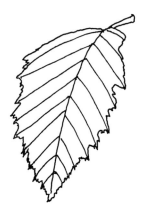

    Alternate leaves are 1½ to 3 inches (38.11 to 76.2 mm) long, with broad, triangular shape tapering to a pointed tip. Edges have both coarse and fine, sharp teeth. Top is dull dark green and underside yellowish green. Veins flare out in almost straight lines from the center vein and are more or less evenly spaced. Tree bark is rough, scaly, and yellow to brown.

AMERICAN ELM page 188

    Alternate, simple leaves are 3 to 5 inches (76.2 to 127 mm) long and double-toothed, with fine teeth between evenly spaced coarse teeth. Leaf base is lopsided, with one side obviously higher than the other. Upper leaf surface is usually smooth but rarely may be rough.

CEDAR ELM page 190

Alternate, small, boat-shaped, double-toothed, leaves are 1 to 2 inches (25.4 to 50.8 mm) long and ½ to 1 inch (12.7 to 25.4 mm) wide. Very rough upper surface and parallel, straight veins. Petiole is ¼ inch (6.4 mm) long and covered with woolly hairs. Twigs are often winged, with two parallel small, narrow, winglike growths.

SEPTEMBER ELM page 192

Alternate arrowhead-shaped leaves are 2 to 3 ½ inches (50.8 to 88.9 mm) long. Lopsided base and leaf blade. Edges are double-toothed. Upper surface may be either smooth or rough. Some twigs and branches have corky growths on four sides.

SLIPPERY ELM page 194

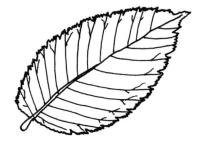

Alternate, double-toothed leaves are 4 to 7 inches (101.6 to 177.8 mm) long and 2 to 3 inches (50.8 to 76.2 mm) wide. Blade is fairly oval, with pointed tip and lopsided base. Upper surface is dull, dark green and sandpaper rough.

WINGED ELM page 196

Alternate, double-toothed leaves are 1½ to 3 inches (38.1 to 76.2 mm) long and 1 to 1½ inches (25.4 to 38.1 mm) wide, with evenly spaced coarse teeth separated by fine ones. One side of leaf is larger than the other, as though the yellow leaf stem is slightly off on one side of the base circle. Upper leaf surface is smooth. There are usually flat-topped corky ridges along the twig between leaves.

HOPHORNBEAM page 228

 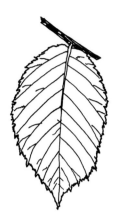

Alternate, simple leaves are 2 to 5 inches (50.8 to 127 mm) long. Generally oblong, with narrowed tip and rounded base. Margins are sharply toothed with small, fine teeth and sometimes doubly toothed with occasional larger, coarse teeth. Top is dull yellow-green and smooth; bottom is pale green and often slightly hairy. Lateral buds are sickle-shaped. Bark is thin, light tan to brown, and shredded.

HORNBEAM page 230

Alternate, simple leaves 2 ½ to 5 inches (63.5 to 127 mm) long. Rounded base and tapered point. Edges are both fine- and coarse-toothed. Dark green above, pale below, and smooth on both surfaces. The bark is smooth and musclelike, dark gray in color.

Blunt-toothed Edges

Compare your sample with the following trees:

Chestnut Oak	*Balsam Poplar*
Chinkapin Oak	*White Poplar*
Swamp Chestnut Oak	*Witchhazel*

CHESTNUT OAK page 304

Alternate, simple, tough-textured, blunt-toothed leaves are 4 to 8 inches (101.6 to 203.2 mm) long, often clustering at ends of branches. Flaring gently from a narrow, tapered base to a broad, rounded tip, each leaf has nine to sixteen pairs of veins that each end in the center of a spiked tooth. Bark is light gray, hard, and deeply fissured. Tree grows on dry sites.

CHINKAPIN OAK page 306

Alternate, tough-textured, yellow-green, glossy leaves are 2 to 6 inches (50.8 to 152.4 mm) long and vary from long to wide, but in all cases are forward-pointing and blunt-toothed. Bark is light gray and very crumbly. Tree is usually found on dry soils.

SWAMP CHESTNUT OAK page 314

 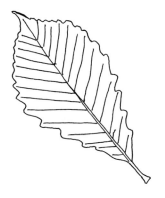

Alternate, simple, rough-textured, blunt-toothed leaves are 4 to 8 inches (101.6 to 203.2 mm) long, often clustering at ends of branches. The edges of the leathery diamond-shaped blade are coarsley wavy-toothed. The smooth top is dark green, the downy bottom, pale. Bark is light gray, sometimes with a pink cast, crumbly, and thin.

BALSAM POPLAR

Alternate, simple leaves are 3 to 6 inches (76.2 to 152.4 mm) long. Broadly rounded or heart-shaped base and long, tapering tip with blunt-toothed edges. Shiny dark green above and paler below, often with rusty hairs along the lower veins. Buds are about 1 inch (25.4 mm) long, orange-brown, curved, resinous, and fragrant. Tree bark is white. Twigs have a bitter, aspirin-like taste. A predominately northern species, it is found throughout Alaska, Canada, and Newfoundland. It also grows in the Rocky Mountains in pockets and in the eastern Appalachians to West Virginia.

WHITE POPLAR page 352

Alternate, simple, blunt-toothed leaves are 2 to 4 inches (50.8 to101.6 mm) long and almost as wide. Dark green upper surface and silvery white, woolly lower surface. Edges are wavy-toothed and often lobed like maple. Petiole is coated with a thick mat of silver-white hairs.

WITCHHAZEL

 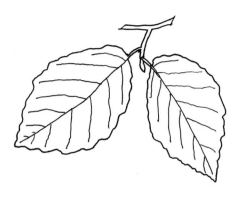

Alternate, simple leaves are 2 ½ to 6 inches (63.5 to 152.4 mm) long and 2 to 3 ½ inches (50.8 to 88.9 mm) wide. Rounded base and pointed tip. Edges have irregularly shaped, blunt teeth. Small tree or shrub. Witchhazel has little value commercially and is seldom used as an ornamental. It has a large range in the eastern and midwestern United States. It is commonly found along the banks of streams, lakes, swamps, and moist forest stands.

SIMPLE ROUNDED LOBES
Compare your sample to the following trees:

Ginkgo	*Overcup Oak*	*Water Oak*
Paper Mulberry	*Post Oak*	*White Oak*
Blackjack Oak	*Sand Post Oak*	*Sassafras*
Bur Oak	*Swamp White Oak*	

GINKGO page 200

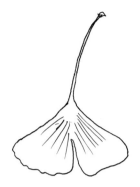

Alternate, simple leaves are 2 to 3 inches (50.8 to 76.2 mm) long and wide, triangular, growing in clusters from short spurs. Leaf flares out in a two-lobed fan shape from narrow beginning point at petiole to wide end that is smooth or sometimes wavy on the edges.

PAPER MULBERRY

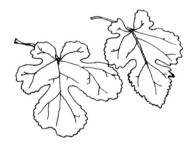

Alternate and occasionally opposite leaves, simple, 3 ½ to 8 inches (88.9 to 203.2 mm) long and almost as wide. Edges are coarsely toothed, with either sharp or blunt teeth, and may have two or more wide lobes separated by deep, rounded sinuses. Upper surface is smooth and deep green; lower surface is a lighter green, with veins covered with hair. Native to China and Japan, the tree has been cultivated in the United States. Mature trees seldom produce fruit but was once grown to produce paper from the inner bark.

BLACKJACK OAK page 276

Alternate, tough, leathery leaves are 4 to 8 inches (101.6 to 203.2 mm) long and wide, with three shallow, broad, bristle-tipped lobes near the end and a narrow but rounded base that may have additional small lobes. Brownish or orangish hairs may be present on lower surface. Tree is usually small and scrubby, with dead limbs, and growing on dry sites.

BUR OAK page 302

 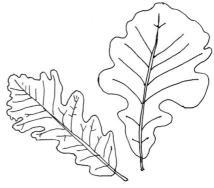

Alternate, tough leaves are usually 6 to 10 inches (152.4 to 254 mm) long. Narrow at the base, with deep, rounded sinuses and lobes, and fat at the top, with shallow, rounded sinuses and lobes. Wings of heavy, dark cork often grow on all sides of the smaller branches.

OVERCUP OAK page 308

Alternate leaves are quite variable but usually are 6 to 8 inches (152.4 to 203.2 mm) long and 1 to 4 inches (25.4 to 101.6 mm) wide, with deep sinuses and five to nine rounded lobes. Base is usually tapered gradually from a thin point to the widest lobes, which occur about midway along the leaf. Thick and leathery, with a bright green top surface and a pale green, sometimes fuzzy bottom. Tree bark is light gray and flaky. Acorn fruits are almost completely enclosed by scaly caps.

POST OAK page 310

Alternate, thick, leathery leaves are 1½ to 6 inches (38.1 to 152.4 mm) long and ¾ to 4 inches (19.1 to 101.6 mm) wide. Tough but distinctive, with cross-shaped look. The two central lobes are noticeably larger than the others. Lower surface is usually covered with star-shaped hairs. Both lobes and sinuses are rounded. Tree can be distinguished from sand post oak by its larger leaves.

SAND POST OAK

 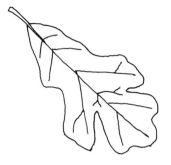

Alternate, thick, leathery leaves are 1½ to 3 inches (38.1 to 76.2 mm) long and ¾ to 1½ inches (19.1 to 38.1 mm) wide. Variable but distinctive cross-shaped lobe patterns. The central and terminal lobes are noticeably larger than the others. Top is smooth, and bottom is usually covered with a heavy mat of hairs that often look solid white when turned toward direct sunlight. Tree can be distinguished from post oak by its smaller, more variable leaves. This scrubby tree is found growing on dry, sandy ridges and pine barrens of the coastal plains and Mississippi River bottoms and is considered a variety of Post Oak.

SWAMP WHITE OAK page 316

Alternate, simple leaves are 4 to 7 inches (101.6 to 177.8 mm) long and 2 to 4½ inches (50.8 to 114.3 mm) wide. Leaves are narrow at the base, widening closer to the center, and tapering back down to a pointed tip. Leaf shapes can vary considerably, with some shallow lobes and sinuses and others with a single, wavy wide lobe on either side. The upper surface is dark glossy green and the lower surface is white with velvety hairs.

WATER OAK page 298

Alternate, simple leaves are very variable in both size and shape. Typically 2 to 4 inches (50.8 to 101.6 mm) long and 1 to 2 inches (25.4 to 50.8 mm) wide, with a thin base that flares out at a long angle a little over half the total length, and then rounds into a wide, irregular end that looks like a duck's track or perhaps a snowshoe. Leaf is usually shallowly three-lobed toward the tip. Thin but firm in texture, dull bluish green on top and pale on the bottom. Small tufts of hair may be found along the veins.

WHITE OAK page 318

Alternate leaves are tough, vary in size and shape but almost always have the same number of lobes on each side. The outside edge is smooth, with the main vein terminating at the end of the center lobe; veins to the other lobes come off different places along the central vein. Ends of lobes are rounded. Sinuses vary in depth, from quite shallow to dipping almost all the way to the midvein. Bottom surface is smooth.

SASSAFRAS page 356

Alternate leaves are 3 to 5 inches (76.2 to 127 mm). Tree may have a mixture of leaves with no lobes, two lobes, and three lobes all growing together in the crown. Edges are smooth, giving the lobed leaves the look of mittens. Crushed leaves have orange peel or root beer smell.

SIMPLE POINTED LOBES
Compare your sample to the following trees:

Red Mulberry	*Northern Red Oak*	*Texas Red Oak*
White Mulberry	*Pin Oak*	*Turkey Oak*
Bear Oak	*Shumard Oak*	*Yellow-Poplar*
Black Oak	*Southern Red Oak*	*Sweetgum*
Cherrybark Oak	*Scarlet Oak*	*Sycamore*

RED MULBERRY page 270

Alternate leaves are 4 to 7 inches (101.6 to 177.8 mm) long and 2 ½ to 5 inches (63.5 to 127 mm) wide. Trees may have leaves with no lobes or a mixture of leaves with no lobes, one lobe, and two lobes all growing on the same tree in two rows per branch. The base of the leaf blade is off-sided, with one side wider than the other. The tips are long and sharply pointed. Upper leaf surface is rough; lower surface is hairy. Edges are coarsely toothed.

WHITE MULBERRY

Alternate, simple leaves are 2 ½ to 7 inches (63.5 to 177.8 mm) long, aligned in two rows along stem. Leaves are broad and variably shaped, with broadly rounded bases, sharp tips, and long stalks. Edges are coarsely toothed and sometimes divided in three to five lobes. Shiny green on top, paler and slightly hairy beneath. Scratching stem releases milky sap. Long berries are edible. Non-native tree.

BEAR OAK page 272

Alternate leaves are 2 to 4 inches (50.8 to 101.6 mm) long and 1½ to 3 inches (38.1 to 76.2 mm) wide, with three to seven lobes (usually five) ending with one to three bristled teeth. The lobes are separated by shallow sinuses. The thick, leathery leaf is dark green above and pale green to gray below with dense hairs. The secondary veins are raised on both surfaces. Fall leaf color is dull red or yellow and the leaves often remain on the tree through winter.

BLACK OAK page 274

Alternate leaves are tough and 4 to 8 inches (101.6 to 203.2 mm) long, with very variable lobes and sinuses. Some sinuses are very shallow, while others are very deep. Lobes have prominent spikes on the tips. Lustrous dark green above and pale yellow-green below. Yellow fuzz can usually be found along lower vein surfaces and sometimes covering the entire bottom. Fall leaf color is bronze.

CHERRYBARK OAK page 278

Alternate, clustered leaves are 3 ½ to 12 inches (88.9 to 304.8 mm) long, 2 ½ to 6 inches (63.5 to 152.4 mm) wide, and of variable size and shape. Margins are smooth. Five to eleven lobes, with the middle lobes usually at right angles to the central vein of the leaf. The lobes are often distinctive, beginning wide at the base, then tapering uniformly to a sharp tip that has one to three bristles. The top is glossy; the bottom is covered with pale gray fuzz. Both the upper and lower secondary veins are raised.

NORTHERN RED OAK page 282

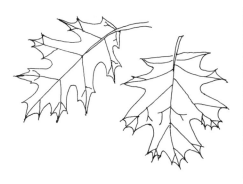  

Alternate leaves are 5 to 8 inches (127 to 203.2 mm) long and 4 to 5 inches (101.6 to 127 mm) wide, with sinuses usually halfway to leaf midrib. Toothed lobes are regularly coarse and point forward at a 45-degree angle toward the end of the leaf. Upper surface is smooth, dull, and dark green to glossy in the western part of the range; bottom is smooth and pale green. There are occasional small hair tufts growing along bottom of veins. Fall leaf color is rusty red. Bark top plates have silver streaks.

PIN OAK page 284

Alternate leaves are tough and 3 to 5 inches (76.2 to 127 mm) long, with five to seven (usually five) prominent, sharply spiked lobes and broad, deep sinuses. Smooth above; small tufts of hair beneath at the vein junctions. Tree limbs are thickly layered, coming out at right angles, with upper limbs pointing upward and lower limbs drooping down toward the ground.

SHUMARD OAK page 290

Alternate leaves are tough and 5 to 7 inches (127 to 177.8 mm) long, with sinuses more than halfway to the midrib. Side ribs angle upward at a 45-degree angle in seven to nine forward-angled, bristle-tipped, coarse-toothed lobes. Lobes on one side of leaf are often off-center from the lobes on the other side of the leaf, with one base lobe wider than the other. Leaf shape and size are very variable.

SOUTHERN RED OAK page 292

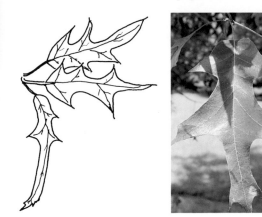 

Alternate leaves are tough and 5 to 7 inches (127 to 177.8 mm) long, with rusty to hairy undersides and two distinct shapes. One resembles a turkey foot, with three lobes and two sinuses; the other is five-lobed, with coarse teeth on the lobes. The base is rounded, and the end lobe is usually the longest in both shapes.

SCARLET OAK page 286

Alternate, lustrous, tough, dark green leaves are 3 to 8 inches (76.2 to 203.2 mm) long, with five to nine long, narrow, toothed, spiked lobes separated by deep, rounded sinuses that extend almost to the midrib. Bottom is smooth except for occasional small tufts of hair along veins. Fall leaf color is burnt to brilliant scarlet red. Trunk bark is silver-streaked. Sap smells like urine.

TEXAS RED OAK page 294

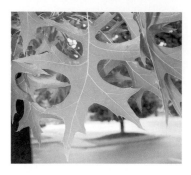 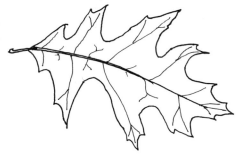

Alternate, simple, thick leaves are 4 to 8 inches (101.6 to 203.2 mm) long and 2 ¼ to 5 ¼ inches (57.2 to 133.4 mm) wide, with a stretched look. The five to seven spike-tipped lobes are narrow, long, and separated by very deep sinuses that often come almost all the way to the leaf's central vein. Top is shiny green. Tufts of orange hair can usually be found on the bottom, growing in the junctions between the central and side veins.

TURKEY OAK page 296

Alternate, simple, thick, shiny leaves are 4 to 8 inches (101.6 to 203.2 mm) long and clustered on branch tips. Leaves have three to five lobes, with the two longest lobes next to the leaf tip and projecting out at almost right angles to the tip, forming what resembles a turkey's footprint. The sinuses are very deep, and the lobes are spike-tipped, each with one to three bristles. Base is sharply angled from the petiole out to the first set of lobes. Veins stand out on both top and bottom surfaces. Occasional tufts of reddish hair can be found along the veins on the bottom. Tree is usually small and scruffy in appearance.

YELLOW-POPLAR   page 396

Alternate leaves are 3 to 8 inches (76.2 to 203.2 mm) long and wide, about the size of a man's hand, with four pointed lobes forming a distinct tulip shape. Central vein ends at the midpoint of the center sinus.

SWEETGUM   page 374

Alternate, simple leaves are 4 to 7 inches (101.6 to 177.8 mm) long and almost that wide. Leaf forms a distinctive five-pointed star shape, with deep, V-shaped sinuses and long, pointed lobes. Finely toothed edges. Shiny, dark green blade has five major veins radiating out from the leaf stalking. Fall leaf color varies from yellow to a deep purplish red.

SYCAMORE   page 376

Alternate, wide, irregularly fan-shaped leaves are 4 to 8 inches (101.6 to 203.2 mm) long, usually slightly longer and wider than a man's hand. Edges are smooth. Smooth top is bright green; bottom is pale green and furry in early summer, becoming smooth later in the season. The usually hairy leaf stalk's hollow base covers the twig bud. Tree has large, greenish gray to silver-white patches of very smooth bark.

Alternate Compound Leaves

1. If your leaf has once-compounded leaves, go to *Alternate Singly Compound Leaves* on page 95.

2. If your leaf is compounded twice, go to *Alternate Doubly Compound Leaves* on page 104.

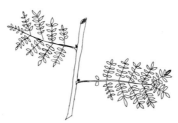

ALTERNATE SINGLY COMPOUND LEAVES
Compare your sample with the following trees:

Ailanthus	*Pignut Hickory*	*Water Hickory*
Butternut	*Red Hickory*	*Black Locust*
Bitternut Hickory	*Sand Hickory*	*Waterlocust*
Pecan (Pecan-	*Shagbark Hickory*	*Mountain-ash*
Hickory Group)	*Shellbark Hickory*	*Black Walnut*
Mockernut Hickory	*Southern Shagbark*	*Yellowwood*
Nutmeg Hickory	*Hickory*	

AILANTHUS page 134

   Alternate, very large leaves are 18 to 36 inches (457.2 to 914.4 mm) long, with eleven to forty-one dark green leaflets that are 2 to 6 inches (50.8 to 152.4 mm) long. Leaflets are narrow and arrowhead-shaped, with a few coarse teeth toward the base. Stem has rank smell when broken. Gray bark is smooth.

BUTTERNUT page 172

 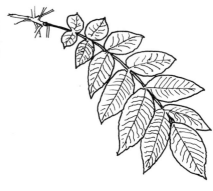

Alternate leaves are 15 to 30 inches (381 to 762 mm) long, with eleven to seventeen leaflets that are 2 to 4 inches (50.8 to 101.6 mm) long. Leaflets are sharply toothed, with pointed tips and broadly pointed to rounded bases. Upper surface is yellowish green and smooth; lower surface is paler and covered with hairs.

BITTERNUT HICKORY page 210

Alternate leaves are 6 to 10 inches (152.4 to 254 mm) long, with seven to eleven narrow leaflets that are 4 to 6 inches (101.6 to 152.4 mm) long. Bright green on top and pale below, with light fuzz on lower surface. Margins are fine- to coarse-toothed. Buds are flat and have a bright, sulfur yellow color.

PECAN page 212

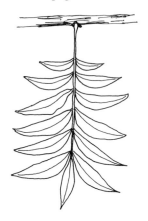  

Alternate, dark yellow-green leaves are 12 to 20 inches (304.8 to 508 mm) long, with eleven to seventeen short-stalked, curved, sharply pointed leaflets that are 3 to 7 inches (76.2 to 177.8 mm) long. Fine teeth along the edges. Leaves cluster at branch ends.

MOCKERNUT HICKORY page 216

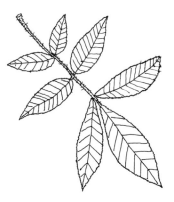 

Alternate, fragrant leaves are 8 to 12 inches (203.2 to 304.8 mm) long with five to nine (usually seven) deep green to yellow-green leaflets. The leaflet bottom and leaf stalk, both petiole and rachis, are covered with fuzz. Edges are fine- to coarse-toothed.

NUTMEG HICKORY

Alternate, compound leaves are 8 to 14 inches (203.2 to 355.6 mm) long, with five to nine broadly spear-shaped, long, slender-tipped leaflets. The terminal leaflet is usually larger than the lateral ones. Lower surface is covered with white to brown scales and fine hairs; upper surface is dark green and shiny. This is a rare tree that is found growing along riverbanks and in southern swamps.

PIGNUT HICKORY page 218

Alternate, compound leaves are 6 to 14 inches (152.4 to 355.6 mm) long, with five to seven leaflets (usually five). Dark green above and pale below. Smooth on both top and bottom, with sharp-toothed edges. Leaf stalk, both petiole and rachis, is smooth. Husk has a smooth surface and cracks halfway down from top to bottom.

RED HICKORY page 220

Alternate, compound leaves are 6 to 14 inches (152.4 to 355.6 mm) long, with five to seven leaflets (usually seven). Dark green above and paler below. Smooth on top and bottom, with sharp-toothed edges. Leaf stalk is smooth. Lumpy nut husk cracks all the way from top to bottom.

SAND HICKORY

Alternate, compound leaves are 7 to 15 inches (177.8 to 381 mm) long, usually with seven leaflets that are 3 ½ to 6 inches (88.9 to 152.4 mm) long, narrow, and finely toothed. Tiny silver or yellowish scales on lower surface cause the bottom of the leaflets to look almost shiny white in sunlight. Leaf stalks are hairy. Twigs and buds may also have silver scales. Also called Pale Hickory, Sand Hickory is found in the southern Piedmont on dry and rocky soils but seldom in any abundance. Often mistaken for other hickories such as Mockernut and Pignut because of the similarities of the leaves and habitat.

SHAGBARK HICKORY page 222

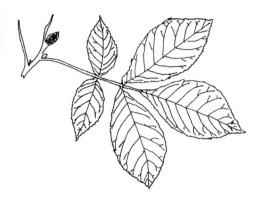

Alternate leaves are 8 to 14 inches (203.2 to 355.6 mm) long, with five to seven finely toothed leaflets. Dark yellow-green above and pale, often fuzzy below, with tufts of white hair on tooth ends. Leaf stem is smooth. Gray, armorlike tree bark peels in long, vertical strips.

SHELLBARK HICKORY page 226

Alternate, large, compound leaves 15 to 24 inches (381 to 609.6 mm) long, with five to nine leaflets (usually seven). Dark green on top, yellow-green and fuzzy below. Stout, buff-colored twigs are covered with orange lines, or lenticels. Gray, armorlike tree bark varies from scruffy to peeling in vertical strips. Large, oblong, slightly flattened nuts are about the same size as extra large hen eggs.

SOUTHERN SHAGBARK HICKORY page 224

Alternate, compound leaves are 6 to 10 inches (152.4 to 254 mm) long and have five sharply toothed leaflets. The slender, spear-shaped leaflets taper to long points and are 4 to 7 inches (101.6 to177.8 mm) long and one-fourth as wide. Teeth along edges are noticeably forward-facing.

WATER HICKORY page 214

Alternate compound leaves are 9 to 15 inches (228.6 to 381 mm) long, with seven to thirteen dark green, narrow, sickle-shaped leaflets growing from short stalks. Leaflets are 2 to 5 inches (50.8 to 127 mm) long and ½ to 1½ inches (12.7 to 38.1 mm) wide, with curved tips and finely toothed edges. Base and tip are both pointed. The fruit is nutlike, with a leathery covering that has four distinctly protruding ridges from base to tip. Tree is found growing in swampy areas.

BLACK LOCUST page 240

Alternate leaves are 6 to 10 inches (152.4 to 254 mm) long, with seven to nineteen small, thin, oval leaflets down two sides of each stalk in a flat pattern. Sharp thorns up to 1 inch (25.4 mm) long may be present along stems and up and down trunk.

WATERLOCUST page 244

 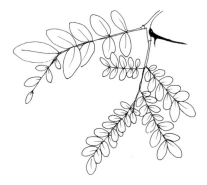

Alternate compound and sometimes doubly compound leaves are 6 to 10 inches (152.4 to 254 mm) long, with twelve to twenty small, long, oval leaflets that are ½ to 1 inch (12.7 to 25.4 mm) long. The leaflet surfaces are dark green to yellow-green above and lighter below. Very large thorns with side thorns are often present on the twigs and trunk. Fruit is a wide, flat bean that is 1 to 3 inches (25.4 to 76.2 mm) long, with a long stem and one to three seeds inside the pod. Tree grows in swampy areas that are underwater much of the year.

MOUNTAIN-ASH

Alternate, compound leaves are 4 to 9 inches (101.6 to 228.6 mm) long, with thirteen to seventeen lance-shaped leaflets that are 1 to 3 inches (25.4 to 76.2 mm) long and finely toothed, starting about one-third of the way from the base. Smooth on top and bottom, with tops being dark yellowish green. In late fall, this small tree has large, showy clusters of red-orange berries that are favored by many birds. It grows both in swamps and high rocky soils in the southern Appalachians and in Labrador and Newfoundland. Often used as an ornamental because of the showy berries.

BLACK WALNUT page 384

Alternate, aromatic leaves are 12 to 24 inches (304.8 to 609.6 mm) long, with thirteen to twenty-three sharply toothed and pointed leaflets that are 2 to 4 inches (50.8 to 101.6 mm) long, of which the terminal leaflet is often missing. Leaflets are smooth on top and bottom. Bark is dark brown to silver-black. Inner bark is dark brown and gives off a faint but distinctive smell when broken.

YELLOWWOOD page 398

 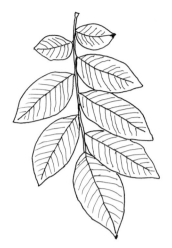

Alternate, compound, smooth-edged leaves are 8 to 12 inches (203.2 to 304.8 mm) long, with seven to eleven boat-shaped, shiny, smooth, green leaflets that are 2 ¼ to 4 inches (57.2 to 101.6 mm) long and 1 to 2 inches (25.4 to 50.8 mm) wide. Leaflets are attached in an alternate pattern. Large leaf stalk base completely covers bud. Branch tip is covered by last leaf node, making last compound leaf look like an extension of the twig. Wood is bright yellow.

ALTERNATE DOUBLY COMPOUND LEAVES
Compare your sample with the following trees:

Albizia   *Kentucky Coffeetree*
Chinaberry   *Honeylocust*
Devil's-Walkingstick

ALBIZIA page 136

Alternate, flattened, blue-green leaves are doubly compound and 6 to 15 inches (152.4 to 381 mm) long. The five to twelve pairs of side stalks are covered with fine hairs, and each has thirty or more closely spaced, fernlike leaflets that fold together along the central vein at night.

CHINABERRY page 182

Alternate, doubly compound leaves are 10 to 20 inches (254 to 508 mm) long, with ragged-looking, arrowhead-shaped leaflets that are 1½ to 2½ inches (38.1 to 63.5 mm) long. Leaflets have long tips and coarsely toothed edges that are sometimes lobed. Both top and bottom surfaces are smooth.

DEVIL'S-WALKINGSTICK

Alternate, doubly compound, and large leaves are 36 inches (914.4 mm) long and 30 inches (762 mm) wide. The numerous leaflets are finely saw-toothed and dark green above and paler beneath. The leaf stalk and plant trunk are both covered with long, sharp thorns in fan-shaped patterns. A shrub or small tree, it is found on moist soils under hardwood stands. Devil's-Walkingstick so named due to its numerous sharp spines.

KENTUCKY COFFEETREE page 238

Alternate, doubly compound leaves are 12 to 24 inches (304.8 to 609.6 mm) long, with rounded leaflets and no thorns on leaf, stem, or tree.

HONEYLOCUST page 242

Alternate, compound and sometimes doubly compound leaves are 6 to 8 inches (152.4 to 203.2 mm) long, with eighteen to twenty-eight small, oval leaflets that are ⅜ to 1¼ inches (9.5 to 31.8 mm) long and smooth on both sides. Blades are shiny dark green above and dull yellow-green below. Very large, strong thorns with side thorns are usually present on the stems and tree trunk.

PART TWO

All-Season Identification

Tree identification can occur in any season. Although distinguishing between types of leaves may be one critical element, it is important to understand that you have more tools at your disposal. This does require getting to know the *whole* tree, so when leaves aren't present proper identification may still be achieved. Other identifying characteristics that aid in distinguishing between species can be found in the bark, trunk, limbs, buds, persistent fruit, and even odors. This section considers these differences.

3

Tree Structure and Life Stages

Every tree has the same basic structure, with a crown, trunk, and root system.

CROWN

A tree's crown, commonly known as the treetop, consists of a group of limbs that support leaf-manufacturing systems. The limb's major job is to place as many leaves as possible in strategic places to receive just the right amount of sunlight to obtain the energy needed to manufacture food for the tree. In hot weather, this includes leaves within the shade of their neighbors, because those receiving direct sunlight get so hot that they shut down to prevent excessive water loss through transpiration out of their lower-surface pores, or stomata.

TRUNK

The trunk is the result of the tree's race for unobstructed sunlight. It gets taller by the very top of the tree elongating upward each spring while dropping off lower limbs. A mark placed on the trunk will not move upward. As the tree gets taller, the trunk also gets thicker to maintain treetop support.

ROOT SYSTEM

More than 90 percent of the average tree's root system is located in the top 18 inches (457.2 mm) of soil. Roots will go wherever they can find air, water, and nutrients from which to manufacture food. All three of these items are most abundant close to the surface, so that is where the majority of the roots go. Most trees lose the taproot—a primary root that extends straight down into the soil—as soon as the lateral root system is established well enough to support the tree.

Root systems usually spread out horizontally far beyond the length of the limbs. As a general rule, the roots can be found one and a half times as far out from the trunk as the longest limbs.

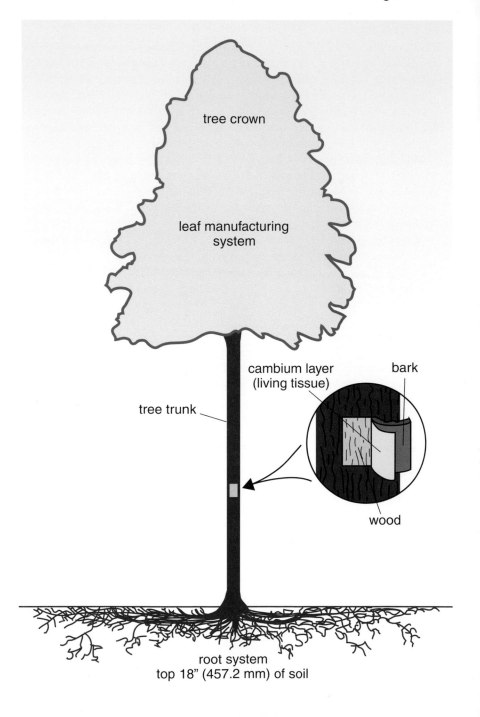

tree crown

leaf manufacturing system

cambium layer (living tissue)

bark

tree trunk

wood

root system
top 18" (457.2 mm) of soil

LIFE STAGES

Trees vary so much in life expectancy that knowing an individual tree's chronological age is not as useful as being able to recognize its current life stage. Once you have determined the tree's stage of life, you can manage it accordingly. Young trees are the most resilient and can be managed the most aggressively. Trees in their prime through old age seldom need our help but may be somewhat forgiving of our actions. Trees that have reached their twilight years will seldom respond to or survive our loving but misguided efforts.

When planning proper management strategies, it helps to remember that the shortest tree life expectancy matches our own, but some trees live over a thousand years. This means that many very old trees will probably outlive us, so there is seldom a reason to make a hurried decision involving the trees that are living around us.

Regardless of their life stage, the worst abuses we can put a tree through are topping the limbs of the crown and burying or trenching through the root system. A good rule of thumb for most established trees is to work under or around the root system and prune only diseased, damaged, or dead limbs. As much as possible, the best tree management is usually to let them grow in peace.

Determining the life stage of a small tree that is overtopped and shaded by its neighbors can be tricky. The tree may be in an advanced life stage even though it is small, or it may be a shade-loving species that is in an early stage of life. The following pictures and descriptions are valid regardless of tree size and situation.

We all begin life as babies.

And soon grow into teenagers.

"Teenage" trees have long, slender branches and pointed tops.

We quickly reach the prime years of our life.

Trees in their prime have full, round-topped crowns filled with long, strong branches.

Only to find ourselves sliding into middle age.

Middle-aged tree crowns flatten out on top as the limbs grow thicker.

All too soon we reach retirement, indicating old age.

Trees sliding into old age have flat-topped crowns filled with heavy limbs that are sometimes covered with short sprouts. Gaps start appearing in the crown as major limb systems die out.

At long last, we sit back and bask in the golden light of our twilight years.

Trees living out their twilight years have small crowns of scattered, large limbs that are often covered with short twigs.

We, like all other living things, eventually die.

4

Quick Winter ID Guide

Tree identification can be challenging any time of the year, but it can be especially so in the winter, when the leaves have dropped off the tree and the remaining buds and twigs are out of reach. The most readily available, accurate clues in winter identification of trees can be found by observing the tree's bark and overall growth characteristics. Looking on the ground beneath the tree for leaves and fruit can also often help with identification, but take care not to misidentify the tree by picking up leaves or fruit from a neighboring tree by mistake.

The goal of this section is to provide a means of identifying the group to which the tree in question belongs, and when possible, to further identify the tree by its specific name. The following quick winter ID guide is given to simplify the identification of trees listed in this section. Check the lists for the characteristics that match your tree in question. Possible trees are given for each description.

BARK CHARACTERISTICS

The bark of different tree species varies widely. It can be smooth, thick and rough, thin and rough, flaky, peeling, scaly, woven, or shredded. Inner bark is a different color and is exposed on some trees.

Smooth Bark

Smooth bark does not have ridges and valleys on the surface.

Pebble surface on thin light gray bark; small tree:
ALBIZIA page 136

Smooth, hard, light gray, young bark with occasional large bumps:
YELLOW BUCKEYE page 170

Smooth, hard, light gray bark with shallow squiggle surface marks:
  AILANTHUS page 134
  PAULOWNIA page 324

Smooth, hard, mouse gray bark, no large warts:
  BEECH page 158
  YELLOWWOOD page 398

Smooth, hard, mouse gray bark with occasional warts:
  HACKBERRY page 202
  SUGARBERRY page 204

Smooth, hard, purple-gray bark with white or tan crevices:
  CAROLINA SILVERBELL page 358

Smooth, tight bark with thick, leathery feel:
  MAGNOLIAS pages 246–257

Smooth, silver-black bark with fine, raised parallel lines and some side peeling in thin strips:
  SWEET BIRCH page 160

Smooth, pale blue-green to white bark with patches of tan bark sloughing off:
  SYCAMORE page 376

Smooth, hard bark, muscle-shaped trunk:
  HORNBEAM page 230

Smooth, green or black bark with blue-white stripes:
  STRIPED MAPLE page 266

Smooth, white bark with black markings:
  ASPENS pages 148–151
  PAPER BIRCH page 162
  WHITE POPLAR page 352
  SYCAMORE page 376

Variable bark, with lower trunk covered in ridges and valleys and smooth upper trunk; smooth portions with pimples:
RED MAPLE page 262

Thick, Rough Bark

Thick, rough bark has a ridge-and-valley pattern where the valleys average more than ½ inch (12.7 mm) deep.

Wide, flat, ash gray ridges divided by wide, rugged, dark chocolate brown valleys:
BUTTERNUT page 172

Dark, almost black bark with silver tinge:
BLACK WALNUT page 384

Light gray, soft, easily broken bark:
WHITE OAKS pages 316–319

Light to very dark gray-brown bark is soft and easily broken:
SWEETGUM page 374
COTTONWOOD page 184

Parallel vertical crevices between flat-topped, sharp-edged bark ridges that may have either an alligator-back or diamond-shaped pattern, light cream-colored inner bark:
ASHES pages 138–147

Light brown bark with parallel, vertical-shaped crevices between flat-topped, round-edged bark ridges; overall look is compressed:
BASSWOODS pages 154–157

Bark looks smooth and flat except for deep, parallel, vertical, knife-blade thin crevices dividing the long, flat-topped plates:
CUCUMBER MAGNOLIA page 248

Dark gray, rough but tight, ridges and valleys:
RED OAKS pages 272–301

Rectangular, thick, shiny, purple to smoke gray bark plates that crack off in paper-thin layers to expose tan inner bark:
MOUNTAIN SILVERBELL page 360

Rectangular to square, dark gray to almost black, very thick, chunky bark plates:
>**PERSIMMON** page 326

Rectangular to square, small chunky bark pattern, brown to dark brown color, small tree:
>**FLOWERING DOGWOOD** page 186

Resin pockets on large, flat bark plates of pine tree:
>**SHORTLEAF PINE** page 342

Very thick-ridged, hard, light gray bark with wide, deep crevices:
>**CHESTNUT OAK** page 304
>**SOURWOOD** page 364

Silver-white chalk dust in bark valleys:
>**YELLOW-POPLAR** page 396
>**COTTONWOOD** page 184

Dark gray to black, rugged bark plates that are as thick as they are long, with horizontal cracks almost as deep as the vertical fissures; small, poorly formed tree:
>**TURKEY OAK** page 296

Thin, Rough Bark
Thin, rough bark may have a wide variety of patterns, including a ridge-and-valley pattern where the valleys average less than ⅜ inch (9.5 mm) deep.

Smooth to slightly fissured, with pink inner mark showing at bottom of each fissure; small tree with broad crown:
>**BEAR OAK** page 272

Long, thin, tight bark plates with both rounded and flat-topped surfaces; bark pattern is very small for size of tree:
>**WATER OAK** page 298

Dark brown bark with long, shallow valleys running vertically between low, tight, almost flat-topped ridges:
>**WILLOW OAK** page 300

Bark is very thin but hard, with long, slightly raised, flat-topped, gray-brown ridges and equally wide, pink to light tan, flat-bottomed valleys of equal width:
PIN OAK page 284

Relatively thin, almost black, rectangular to roughly squared bark plate pattern on round, tall trunk:
CHERRYBARK OAK page 278

Gray bark with randomly placed, variably long, flat-topped bark plates lying on and between wide, shallow, flat-bottomed valleys:
CHINABERRY page 182

Silver streaks on top of bark plates, pruned cleanly, no sap smell:
NORTHERN RED OAK page 282
SHUMARD OAK page 290

Silver streaks on top of bark plates, retained dead branches, fresh sap releases a strong, urinelike odor:
SCARLET OAK page 286

Relatively short and wide, very rough, lumpy bark plates with occasional silver flakes on surface:
BLACKJACK OAK page 276

Thin, gray bark armed with long, slender thorns:
WATERLOCUST page 244

Tree has both smooth bark and thin, flat-topped bark plates separated by long, thin, shallow furrows:
RED MAPLE page 262

Thin but rough-textured bark that looks glued onto the tree:
RED OAKS pages 272–301

Silver-white chalky dust in bark cracks:
YELLOW-POPLAR page 396
EASTERN COTTONWOOD page 184

Silver-gray to reddish brown, thin, wide, flat-topped, rough-edged bark plates with rounded edges and few recognizable crevices:
SLIPPERY ELM page 194
YELLOW BUCKEYE page 170

Flaky Bark
Various bark thicknesses flake off easily when chipped with fingernail.

Bark looks as if it has glued-on silver-black cornflakes:
BLACK CHERRY page 178

Flaking, irregular, disk-shaped patches of thin bark:
YELLOW BUCKEYE page 170

Flaky, silver-gray bark with ridge-and-valley pattern; smooth patches have indented straight lines forming large, triangular shapes:
PECAN page 212

Flaky, grayish brown bark plates with rounded bottom edges:
SMOKETREE page 362

Rectangular, thick, shiny, purple to smoke gray bark plates that crack off in paper-thin layers to expose tan inner bark:
MOUNTAIN SILVERBELL page 360

Flaky, dark bark looks like whipped icing on tall cake:
WHITE WILLOW page 394

Almost white to dark gray, flaky bark may peel from side (dry sites):
WHITE OAK page 318

Almost white to dark gray, flaky bark may peel from side (wet sites) and often has salmon pink glow:
SWAMP CHESTNUT OAK page 314

Almost white to light tan, flaky bark with limbs that turn sharply upward:
CHINKAPIN OAK page 306

Peeling Bark
Bark plates break loose and curl up from the top, bottom, or either side.

Thin yellow bark peeling from side:
> **YELLOW BIRCH** page 166

Thick brown bark peeling from side:
> **RIVER BIRCH** page 164

Purplish gray bark peeling from top and bottom, small tree with short trunk:
> **REDBUD** page 354

Bark peeling from top and bottom, peel ring around base:
> **SILVER MAPLE** page 264

Hard, armorlike bark peeling in strips from top, bottom, or both:
> **SHAGBARK HICKORY** 222
> **SOUTHERN SHAGBARK HICKORY** page 224
> **SHELLBARK HICKORY** page 226

Hard, tough-to-break, gray to black bark peeling from side in long ridges:
> **SUGAR MAPLE** page 268

Bark peeling from side in long, thick, flat-topped plates:
> **BLACK MAPLE** page 258

Thin, smooth, cinnamon to reddish brown bark peeling from side in thin curls:
> **PAPERBARK MAPLE** page 260

Scaly Bark
Thin bark plates crack loose from one or more sides without curling.

Roughly rectangular, sliver-gray, flat, scaly bark plates cracking off from side, often exposing smooth, brown inner bark:
> **HORSECHESTNUT** page 232

Scaling large patches of thin, tan bark revealing large, smooth, pale blue-green or silver-gray patches:
> **SYCAMORE** page 376

Mottled gray, wide, thin, flat, soft, corky, scaly plates:
BLACK ASH page 138

Thin, dark gray bark with purple cast peeling from bottom and sides; small tree with rounded crown:
REDBUD page 354

Light gray bark peeling from side in long, soft, easy-to-break ridges (upland sites):
WHITE OAK page 318

Light gray bark that often has a salmon pink cast, peeling from side in long, soft, easy-to-break ridges (wet areas):
SWAMP CHESTNUT OAK page 314

Flat-topped plates of various lengths that sometimes overlap and other times split into two plates with short cracks between:
RED MULBERRY page 270

Woven Bark
Bark plates are interlaced, with depressions inside the pattern formed by the raised bark. The pattern may be netlike or a long, interlocking ridge-and-valley pattern.

Light brown to silver-gray, flat-topped, diamond-shaped woven bark pattern:
ASHES pages 138–147

Yellow-brown to silver-black, thick, ropelike woven bark:
BLACK LOCUST page 240

Netlike, woven, thin and smooth to almost shaggy, gray bark:
HICKORIES pages 216–227

Netlike, woven, thin and smooth bark pattern; branches grow from trunk smoothly:
BITTERNUT HICKORY page 210

Netlike, woven, thin and smooth bark pattern, with a set of frown lines coming down from each side of branches:
MOCKERNUT HICKORY page 216

Broken net pattern with fairly wide ridges:
   PIGNUT HICKORY page 218

Woven net pattern looks roughly frayed:
   RED HICKORY page 220

Shredded Bark
Bark breaks loose in thin shreds, often giving the surface a fuzzy look.

Thin, shredded, light tan to reddish pink bark with silver-gray highlight strands and evergreen, scalelike needles:
   WHITE CEDARS pages 386–389

Shredded, light gray-brown bark on often-crooked small tree:
   HOPHORNBEAM page 228

Shredded, reddish brown bark; large tree with swollen, fluted base growing in or around water:
   BALDCYPRESS page 152
   PONDCYPRESS page 350

Shredded, reddish brown bark; flat, evergreen needles each with two parallel blue lines along the bottom:
   HEMLOCKS pages 206–209

Shredded bark; evergreen palm leaves growing from top:
   SABAL PALMETTO page 322

Exposed Inner Bark
Bark color changes in valleys and beneath plate surface.

Exposed inner bark reveals chocolate brown inner bark:
   BLACK WALNUT page 384

Exposed inner bark reveals dark reddish brown inner bark with parallel thin white lines:
   ELMS pages 188–197

Exposed inner bark reveals light cream to tan inner bark:
   ASHES pages 138–147
   BOXELDER page 168

Exposed inner bark reveals odorless pale orange inner bark:
OSAGE-ORANGE page 320

Exposed inner bark reveals pale orange inner bark and releases root beer odor:
SASSAFRAS page 356

Pink inner bark shows in bottom of bark cracks:
BEAR OAK page 272
PIN OAK page 284

Gray and purple smooth outer bark with light tan valleys:
CAROLINA SILVERBELL page 358

TREE TRUNK CHARACTERISTICS
Characteristics of the trunk other than the bark can aid in tree identification.

Swollen, deeply fluted trunk base:
BALDCYPRESS page 152
PONDCYPRESS page 350

Swollen, fluted, triangular or square trunk base:
CEDAR ELM page 190

Small to medium-size evergreen with scaly leaves and fluted base:
WHITE CEDARS pages 386–389

Swollen, distorted, diseased trunk base:
SCARLET OAK page 286

Swollen base, often with moss line, light gray, tight, flaky, ridge-and-valley bark pattern (wet areas):
OVERCUP OAK page 308

Swollen base and quickly tapering trunk with chunky, rectangular bark pattern (wet areas):
WATER TUPELO page 382

Smooth patches on bark near base of tree; otherwise rough, light to dark gray bark with long, horizontal pattern, distorted limbs:
POST OAK page 310

Short trunk holding up wide, rounded crown of limbs:
RED MULBERRY page 270

Short, stout, scattered thorns growing from trunk bark:
BLACK LOCUST page 240

Long thorns often with a secondary thorn at base growing from trunk:
HONEYLOCUST page 242
WATERLOCUST page 244

LIMB CHARACTERISTICS

The shape, form, bark pattern, or other unique characteristics of the limbs can help identify the tree.

Tree has light gray to white, flaky bark; limbs turn sharply upward:
CHINKAPIN OAK page 306

Upward-reaching, vase-shaped crown of branches with clusters of fine branch tips that make the tree look as if it is wearing hair nets:
AMERICAN ELM page 188

Large, strong, well-spaced limbs:
COTTONWOOD page 184
RED OAKS pages 272–301
WHITE OAKS pages 302–319
SYCAMORE page 376

Closely spaced, small branches growing from tree at right angles:
RED OAKS pages 272–301
TUPELOS pages 378–383
SWEETGUM page 374

Twisted, unkempt-looking limbs:
CATALPAS pages 174–177
OSAGE-ORANGE page 320
TUPELOS pages 378–383
SASSAFRAS page 356
WILLOWS pages 390–395

Irregularly shaped, open crown of crooked branches, usually with dead branches present:
  BLACKJACK OAK page 276

Large, scattered, twisted limbs with dangling tips that make the tree look as if it were designed for a horror movie:
  POST OAK page 310

Twisted, arched branches with long, slender, beanlike fruit hanging through winter:
  CATALPAS pages 174–177

Short trunk; crown filled with long, strong limbs forming round top:
  RED MULBERRY page 270

Branches from trunk in wagon-wheel whorls:
  AUSTRIAN PINE page 328
  RED PINE page 340
  EASTERN WHITE PINE page 330

Tall central stem with a single cluster of upturned branches surrounding the central stem; all surrounding branches come off the trunk at the same height in a whorl:
  GINKGO page 200

Corky ridges on two sides of small branches, round treetop:
  WINGED ELM page 196

Corky ridges on two sides of small branches, pointed treetop:
  SWEETGUM page 374

Heavy cork on all sides of small branches:
  BUR OAK page 302
  KENTUCKY COFFEETREE page 238

Small, corky ridges on four sides of small branches:
  SEPTEMBER ELM page 192

Branches, twigs, and buds opposite one another:
    ASHES pages 138–147
    BOXELDER page 168
    DOGWOOD page 186
    HORSECHESTNUT page 232
    MAPLES pages 258–269
    YELLOW BUCKEYE page 170

Long, slender, smooth, green twigs:
    BOXELDER page 168

Long, slender, smooth, green twigs with occasional tan, corky warts:
    SASSAFRAS page 356

Long, bright, smooth, burnt orange to yellow, shiny twigs:
    WILLOWS pages 390–395

Very long, slender, graceful twigs hanging straight down:
    WEEPING WILLOW page 392

Square twigs:
    BLUE ASH page 140

Stout thorns growing at leaf junction points on arched branches and twigs:
    OSAGE-ORANGE page 320

Short thorns growing along twig:
    BLACK LOCUST page 240

Long, stout thorns with thumblike spike at base growing along twig:
    HONEYLOCUST page 242
    WATERLOCUST page 244

Well-spaced twig stubs ½ to 1 inch (12.7 to 25.4 mm) long growing along small branches and twigs; clustered leaf scars on stub ends:
    GINKGO page 200

White sap oozes from broken twig:
    RED MULBERRY page 270

CHARACTERISTIC ODORS

Some trees can be identified by a characteristic odor that is released if you break or scratch the twigs or crush the leaf.

Rank odor released by breaking or scratching blunt twigs:
AILANTHUS page 134

Scratched twigs release wintergreen odor:
SWEET BIRCH page 160
YELLOW BIRCH page 166

Scratched slender twigs release pungent odor:
BLACK CHERRY page 178

Scratched twigs release a spicy-sweet odor:
CUCUMBER MAGNOLIA page 248

Pleasant odor is released by scraping twigs; root beer odor released from cut bark:
SASSAFRAS page 356

Crushed leaf releases cherry odor:
CAROLINA CHERRYLAUREL page 180

BUDS

Several trees have distinctive buds that can aid in identification.

Large, shiny, sticky buds:
HORSECHESTNUT page 232

Sulfur yellow buds:
BITTERNUT HICKORY page 210

Long terminal bud covered with white hairs:
BIGLEAF MAGNOLIA page 246

Long, purple bud with crooked tip:
FRASER MAGNOLIA page 250

Long, large, bronze green terminal bud:
   UMBRELLA MAGNOLIA page 256

EVERGREEN TREE CHARACTERISTICS
Evergreen trees have their own unique characteristics that you can often use to tell them apart.

Soft, lacy appearance with filtered light through evergreen needles; dead limbs retained on trunk:
   VIRGINIA PINE page 348

Bundles of needles seem to be sitting on top of branch as though they are being held in the palm of the hand:
   SHORTLEAF PINE page 342

Pine needles growing directly out of tree trunk:
   PITCH PINE page 338

Pine needles form clusters on twigs at the end of the branch, with needles surrounding the branch forming what look like soft needle balls attached in the center by the brown branch:
   LOBLOLLY PINE page 334

Pine needles bunched at end of orange branch, resembling a broom:
   SLASH PINE page 344

Silver flashes in canopy when sun hits silver-haired buds:
   LONGLEAF PINE page 336

PERSISTENT FRUIT
Some tree fruits persist in part or whole into late winter, making them available as a supplemental means of identification.

Large clusters of light tan, paperlike, winged fruit in treetop:
   AILANTHUS page 134

Long, flat, beanlike fruit hanging from branches:
   ALBIZIA page 136
   BLACK LOCUST page 240
   HONEYLOCUST page 242
   REDBUD page 354

Clusters of pea-size berries dangling like spread fingers from the center of small, elbow-shaped wings that are attached to twigs:
   BASSWOODS pages 154–157

Dark brown, heavily treaded, golf-ball-size nuts that may be covered with soft, rotting green or black husks:
   BLACK WALNUT page 384

Heavily treaded nuts the size and shape of goose eggs, covered by furry, sticky, green to black husks:
   BUTTERNUT page 172

Shiny, brown, ½-inch (12.7 mm)-diameter nuts each with a large, tan eye:
   BUCKEYE page 170

Long, pencil-shaped fruit pods that may be split open, releasing white, feathery winged fruit, hanging from twisted arching branches:
   CATALPAS pages 174–177

Light tan, four-ridged nuts, ½ to 2 inches (12.7 to 50.8 mm) in diameter, with hard, dark green to black, round husks usually broken into quarters:
   HICKORIES pages 216–227

Hickory nut husks the size of goose eggs:
   SHELLBARK HICKORY page 226

Burnt red, thick, fleshy, bean pods, 4 to 7 inches (101.6 to 177.8 mm) long by 1½ to 2 inches (38.1 to 50.8 mm) wide:
   KENTUCKY COFFEETREE page 238

Burnt red, flat, beanlike fruit, 1 to 3 inches (25.4 to 76.2 mm) long by 1 inch (25.4 mm) wide:
   WATERLOCUST page 244

Dark brown, stalked fruit pods the size and shape of goose eggs, filled with open cavities from which red seeds are released:
   MAGNOLIAS pages 246–257

Acorn nuts and caps of various shapes, sizes, and descriptions:
   OAKS pages 272–319

Textured, ball-like fruit is 3½ to 5 inches (88.9 to 127 mm) in diameter, lime green, turning black and shriveling up through the winter:
   OSAGE-ORANGE page 320

Large clusters of dangling, golf-ball-size, woodlike, hollow seedpods, usually cracking open from pod tip to release tiny seeds:
   PAULOWNIA page 324

Pinecones of various sizes:
   PINES pages 328–349

Pinecones armed with thick rhinoceros-horn-shaped barbs on scales (higher elevations):
   TABLE MOUNTAIN PINE page 346

Drooping clusters of small, light tan, fine-textured, five-sided seedpods:
   SOURWOOD page 364

PART THREE

Species Accounts

Various identifying characteristics have been explored. Here we consider the *whole* tree as the sum of its parts. Our goal to properly make the correct identification finally must consider the complete tree. The following measurements, detailed descriptions, features, and natural range considerations supplemented with photographs provide the tools necessary to make a positive identification.

AILANTHUS

Ailanthus, *Ailanthus altissima*
Chinese Sumac, Copal-Tree, Paradise-Tree, Tree-of-Heaven

Ailanthus is a medium-size introduced tree that often reaches 50 to 80 feet (15.2 to 24.4 m) in height and 12 to 24 inches (304.8 to 609.6 mm) in diameter at breast height. Its tall, smooth, limb-free trunk and very thin, tight, light gray bark can help identify it. The bark surface is marked with a series of very shallow, light-colored, short, squiggly valleys running up and down the trunk. Large, white splotches may also be found spattered up and down the trunk. Branches usually begin high in the tree. They are big, crooked, blunt-ended, and covered with very large smiley-face leaf scars. When bent, the limbs break off clean, releasing a pungent odor.

The very large compound leaves of Ailanthus (page 95) are 18 to 36 inches (457.2 to 914.4 mm) long, with long opposite rows of eleven to forty-one dark green leaflets that are each 2 to 6 inches (50.8 to 152.4 mm) long. Each leaflet may have a few coarse teeth toward the base. Winged fruit borne in large, tan to burnt red clusters is retained throughout most of the winter.

Features: Aggressively planted during the 1800s as a wonder tree because of its fast growth and ability to live almost anywhere, it has escaped cultivation and in some areas is now considered a weed and a serious pest. As a result of root sprouting and fertile windborne seeds, Ailanthus is often found growing in pure clumps or even extended pure stands.

Natural Range: Although native to China, Ailanthus has become naturalized in many parts of the United States and can be found growing in both urban and forest environments throughout the eastern part of the country.

ALBIZIA

Albizia, *Albizia julibrissin*
Mimosa, Silk-Tree

Albizia is a small introduced tree that seldom grows taller than 25 feet (7.6 m) in height and 10 inches (254 mm) in diameter at breast height. Albizia usually forks low to the ground and forms a wide, flat-topped crown filled with well-spaced, arching branches. The light gray bark is thin and tight, with slightly raised horizontal bumps that give the bark a pebbly feel to the touch. Older trees develop a very shallow ridge-and-valley bark pattern with light tan valleys that are little more than vertical marks.

Albizia leaves (page 105) are alternate, doubly compound, flattened, and blue-green. The main stalk is 6 to 15 inches (152.4 to 381 mm) long, with five to twelve pairs of right-angled side stalks that are covered with fine hairs. Each side stalk holds thirty or more closely spaced, fernlike leaflets that fold together along the central vein at night. Flowers are white and pink puffs of fine-stranded hairs. Long, flat, beanlike fruit develops in late summer and hangs on the tree most of the winter.

Features: Albizia was popular as a featured urban plant for almost two hundred years, but it is in decline because of a deadly wilt disease that is decimating its numbers.

Natural Range: Albizia is an exotic tree native to central China through Iran. It was first introduced into the United States in the mid-1700s. Over time it escaped and became naturalized from Maryland and Indiana in the north to south Florida and east Texas in the south.

ASH

Black Ash, *Fraxinus nigra*
Basket Ash, Brown Ash, Hoop Ash, Swamp Ash, Water Ash

Black Ash is a slow-growing, small to medium-size tree that usually reaches no more than 60 to 70 feet (18.3 to 21.3 m) tall and 12 to 24 inches (304.8 to 609.6 mm) in diameter at breast height. It is most commonly found growing in and around northern bogs and frequently flooded river bottoms. The tree is usually slightly crooked, supporting a tall, open crown of short limbs. The bark is a mottled dark gray. The bark on young trees is smooth, but as the tree matures, it develops wide, flat, scaly plates that are divided from one another by shallow cracks. The bark is soft and corky to the touch, rubbing off easily when brushed over with the hand. The terminal bud is large, brown, and pyramid-shaped. The brown side buds are much smaller and sit on top of the leaf-twig junction on the stem. Leaf scars look like upside-down flat tires. They are rounded everywhere except at the very top, where they flatten out just below the bud.

Opposite, compound leaves (page 36) are 10 to 17 inches (254 to 431.8 mm) long, with seven to eleven (usually nine) finely sawtooth-edged leaflets that are 3 to 5 inches (76.2 to 127 mm) long. The blades are directly attached to the central leaf stalk (petiole and rachis). The individual leaflets do not have stalks. Light tan, single-winged seeds from 1 to 1½ inches (25.4 to 38.1 mm) long are produced in the fall and hang in bunches. The tapered wings extend halfway up the sides of the seed cavities.

Features: Black Ash has been used for centuries to make woven baskets, barrel hoops, and chair bottoms. The seeds are an important source of food for birds and small mammals. Larger species, such as deer and moose, browse on the leaves and twigs. The tree gets its name from its dark heartwood.

Natural Range: Black Ash is our northernmost ash tree. It can be found growing in bogs, swamps, and river bottoms from Canada and New England southward to northern Iowa, Indiana, Ohio, West Virginia, and Pennsylvania.

Blue Ash, *Fraxinus quadrangulata*

Blue Ash is usually a medium-size tree, often reaching 50 to 70 feet (15.2 to 21.3 m) in height and 18 to 36 inches (457.2 to 914.4 mm) in diameter at breast height, but in the best growing conditions, it has the potential to grow much larger. It is a straight tree with slender, right-angled, opposite branches forming a narrowly round crown. The bark of Blue Ash is soft, gray, and flaky, with parallel cracks. Breaking off the surface bark will reveal a light tan inner bark that often has a pinkish overtone. As the tree matures, the bark plates widen and often take on a shingled look. Twigs are perhaps the quickest way to identify Blue Ash in all seasons of the year. The rather stout twigs are square and often have small wings on the four corner angles.

Blue Ash leaves (page 36) are opposite, deciduous, and compound. They range in size from 8 to 12 inches (203.2 to 304.8 mm) long, having seven to eleven stalked leaflets that are 3 to 5 inches (76.2 to 127 mm) long and 1 to 2 inches (25.4 to 50.8 mm) wide. Leaflet blade shape is variable, ranging from long and narrow with a slender tip to wide and rounded at the tip. Blade margins are sharply toothed with fine teeth. Both the upper and lower leaf blade surfaces are smooth, but there are tufts of hair along the veins on the lower surface. The seeds have wings beginning above the midpoint and then growing down the sides and off the tips to form single-bladed wings.

Features: Pioneers used Blue Ash as a source of blue dye by soaking the inner bark in water, giving the tree its name. When the sap from the bark is exposed to light, it turns blue. Today the wood is harvested commercially and marketed as white ash. In the fall, wildlife feed on the seeds.

Natural Range: Blue Ash is not common throughout its range, but it can be found growing in the central portion of the eastern United States, from southern Wisconsin, Indiana, and Ohio southward to northern Mississippi, Alabama, and northwestern Georgia.

Green Ash, *Fraxinus pennsylvanica*
Red Ash, Swamp Ash, Water Ash

Green Ash is a medium to large bottomland tree that seldom matures larger than 60 feet (18.3 m) in height and 18 to 24 inches (457.2 to 609.6 mm) in diameter at breast height in the north, but it may grow twice that large in southern bottomlands. On most sites, it usually develops a long, clean trunk and an oval to rounded top. The tree can often be identified by the presence of large buds sitting on top of the leaf-stem junction. When the leaves are missing, the Green Ash can still be identified by the flat-topped leaf scar with a bud sitting just above it. The twigs are smooth and hairless.

The silver-gray bark pattern of Green Ash is quite variable, from a diamond-shaped, laced pattern with narrow, winding, flat-topped ridges and scalloped valleys to an alligator-back pattern of square, flat-topped plates that are separated vertically by deep cracks and horizontally by shallow cross cracks. Sometimes both bark patterns will be present on the same tree. The trees consistently have a cream-colored inner bark that is easily exposed by breaking off the surface bark. From a distance, the surface of the trunk on all but the largest Green Ash trees looks very tight and uniformly flat on top, regardless of the pattern displayed. Green Ash leaves (page 37) are opposite, compound, blue-green, and 8 to 12 inches (203.2 to 304.8 mm) long. They have three to seven leaflets that are 2 to 5 inches (50.8 to 127 mm) long, with fine- or shallow-toothed edges. Single-winged seeds, with the wing edges extending up the sides, grow in clusters and mature in the fall.

Features: Green Ash wood is harvested and sold as white ash on the commercial market. It is also widely planted as a shade tree and for reclamation in a wide variety of soils. Some taxonomists treat Green Ash and Red Ash as one species, calling Red Ash the hairy form of Green Ash.

Natural Range: Green Ash is a bottomland tree that grows naturally along river bottoms and in low, damp areas throughout the eastern United States.

Red Ash, *Fraxinus pennsylvanica*
Green Ash

Red Ash is a medium-size tree that usually grows 40 to 60 feet (12.2 to 18.3 m) tall and less than 2 feet (.6 m) in diameter, but it occasionally grows over 80 feet (24.4 m) tall and 36 inches (914.4 mm) in diameter at breast height. It is a bottomland tree that is most often found growing along streambanks and in wet areas. The bark is very variable. Sometimes it has long, narrow, curvy ridges that often split into two ridges separated by V-shaped valleys. Bark in this pattern can be quite thick, with rough, rounded bark tops. Other trees may have an alligator-back pattern of blocks that are separated by deep, narrow vertical cracks and horizontal cracks that are only half as deep. The inner bark for both patterns is a pale tan color. Limbs and twigs grow opposite one another. New-growth twigs are covered with very small, white, downy hairs that give them a velvet feel.

Red Ash leaves (page 38) are opposite and compound, 8 to 12 inches (203.2 to 304.8 mm) long, with three to seven leaflets. Leaflet edges may be either smooth or toothed. The leaf stalk and underside of the leaflets are covered with tiny white hairs, giving them downy surfaces that feel silky. Buds are rusty brown, with the end buds much larger than those on the sides of the twigs. The side buds are partially buried in the crotches between the twigs and leaf nodes. Approximately half of the bud protrudes out of the crotch. When the leaves fall, the leaf scars are curved across the top.

Features: Red Ash has long, straight-grained wood that is marketed as white ash and used for manufacturing a wide variety of products. Many forms of wildlife eat the seeds. It is sometimes marketed as Green Ash and planted on a wide variety of sites, where it does well in spite of its preference for wet sites. Many taxonomists list Red Ash as a hairy form of Green Ash.

Natural Range: Red Ash grows in wet areas from Canada to northern Mississippi, Alabama, and Georgia.

White Ash, *Fraxinus americana*
Biltmore Ash, Biltmore White Ash

White Ash is a large tree with the potential for mature heights exceeding 100 feet (30.5 m) and diameters of more than 3 feet (.9 m) at breast height. Trees grown in forested situations are tall and slender, with limb-free trunks and small, oval tops. Trees in open areas tend to be much shorter, with wide, rounded crowns that often hang close to the ground. The limbs, twigs, and leaves all grow opposite one another. The large, blunt-tipped twigs will be smooth and bare unless the tree is the rare Biltmore Ash (page 35) form of White Ash, whose twigs and leaves are covered with tiny, silky smooth, white hairs.

The silver-gray bark of White Ash may have either a diamond-shaped, laced pattern with narrow, winding flat-topped, sharp-edged ridges and deep, scalloped valleys or an alligator-back pattern of square, flat-topped plates that are separated vertically by deep cracks and horizontally by shallow cross cracks. Sometimes both patterns will be present on the same tree. In any case, the top of both patterns is flat and uniform in height, giving the tree a very tight, clean appearance. Breaking or crumbling off the surface bark will expose a cream-colored inner bark.

White Ash leaves (page 39) are opposite, compound, blue-green, and 8 to 12 inches (203.2 to 304.8 mm) long, with five to nine (usually seven) smooth-edged leaflets growing along the sides and end of the leaf stem. When the leaves and buds are within reach, the buried buds in the leaf-limb crotches can identify White Ash. If the leaves are gone, the deeply notched horseshoe-shaped leaf scars that wrap around at least the bottom half of the buds will accomplish the same purpose. In the fall, a single wing is attached to the bottom of the swollen seedpod but does not run up the sides of the pod.

Features: White Ash is commercially harvested and marketed for many wood-related products. It is also widely planted as a shade tree.

Natural Range: White Ash grows throughout the eastern United States in a wide variety of well-drained to dry sites.

ASPEN

Bigtooth Aspen, *Populus grandidentata*
Largetooth Aspen, Popple, Poplar

Bigtooth Aspen is a small to medium-size tree that seldom grows over 40 feet (12.2 m) tall and 1 ⅓ feet (.4 m) in diameter at breast height, but it may occasionally grow much larger. It can be easily identified as a member of the aspens by looking at its various unique bark characteristics. With the exception of the lower 2 feet (.6 m) of the tree, which may be dark and furrowed, the bark is noticeably light gray to almost white. Narrow, dark gray, horizontal lines can be found at random places up and down the tree. On larger trees, these lines are raised, as are scattered small, rough-surfaced bumps. Looking at limb junctures often reveals dark marks drooping down the bark on either side of the limb like dark mustaches or triangles. The bark does not peel away from the trunk.

The winter features of Bigtooth Aspen and Quaking Aspen are so similar that distinguishing the two trees from one another with certainty usually involves finding leaves on the ground and checking the teeth along the blade edges. The leaf blades of Bigtooth Aspen (page 66) are from 2 ½ to 4 inches (63.5 to 101.6 mm) long and broadly arrowhead-shaped, with coarse teeth along the edges, whereas Quaking Aspen leaves have evenly spaced fine teeth. They are smooth on top and hairy on the bottom. The petiole is about the same length as the blade and noticeably flattened.

Features: The wood of the Bigtooth Aspen is used for paper by the forest products industry. The tree is heavily browsed by wildlife, and its bark is a favored food for beavers. It is occasionally planted as a featured yard tree

Natural Range: Bigtooth Aspen ranges from New England and the Great Lakes states southward down through the Cumberland Plateau and Appalachian Mountains of North Carolina, Tennessee, and northern Georgia.

Quaking Aspen, *Populus tremuloides*
Golden Aspen, Mountain Aspen, Poplar, Popple, Trembling Aspen

Quaking Aspen is a small to medium-size tree usually not growing larger than 30 to 40 feet (9.1 to 12.2 m) in height and ⅔ to 1 ⅓ feet (.2 to .4 m) in diameter at breast height, but occasionally it may grow much larger. It can be easily identified as a member of the aspens by looking at its various unique bark characteristics. With the exception of the lower 2 feet (.6 m) of the tree, which may be dark and furrowed, the bark is noticeably light gray to almost white. Narrow, dark gray, horizontal lines can be found at random places up and down the tree. On larger trees, these lines are raised, as are scattered small, rough-surfaced bumps. Looking at limb junctures often reveals dark marks drooping down the bark on either side of the limb like dark mustaches or triangles. The bark does not peel. Limbs are small, pointing slightly upward and forming a long, narrow crown that reaches from the ground to the top in open areas and the upper third of the tree's total height in forested settings.

The winter features of Quaking Aspen and Bigtooth Aspen are so similar that distinguishing the two trees from one another in areas where they grow together usually involves finding leaves on the ground and checking the teeth along the blade edges. The leaf blades of Quaking Aspen (page 58) are from 1 to 2 inches (25.4 to 50.8 mm) long and wide; they are quite round, with three main veins radiating from the base. The margins are broken with regularly spaced fine teeth. The petiole is about the same length as the blade and is flattened on two sides, allowing the leaf to tremble in the slightest of breezes.

Features: The forest industry uses the Quaking Aspen for paper and many other wood-related products. It is browsed by wildlife and occasionally planted as a featured yard tree.

Natural Range: In the eastern United States, Quaking Aspen grows throughout New England and the Great Lakes states. It is one of the most widespread trees in America, also covering much of Canada and the western United States.

BALDCYPRESS

Baldcypress, *Taxodium distichum*

Baldcypress is a large tree that may reach mature sizes of 100 to 150 feet (30.5 to 45.7 m) in height and 3 to 6 feet (.9 to 1.8 m) in diameter at breast height. It is usually found growing around or in water and surrounded by knees, knoblike projections sticking up out of the ground or water. A young tree forms a tall, slender teepee shape. As the tree ages, the lower branches drop off and the crown flattens out. The base of the trunk also swells and becomes deeply fluted, with rounded ridges and deep, narrow fissures. Bark is thin and reddish brown to tan on the young tree, becoming thick and fibrous as the tree ages.

The sharp-tipped, needlelike leaves (page 15) are ½ to ¾ inch (12.7 to 19.1 mm) long and two-ranked, growing featherlike in parallel rows along lateral branches. They are lime green to yellow-green. In the fall, they turn yellow then dull red and drop off, leaving short, thin, reddish brown twigs lined with leaf scars and protruding hard, round leaf buds that make the tree look like a dead evergreen. Round, gumball-size, silver-gray fruit balls develop over the summer. They open to release seeds in fall and drop off the tree soon after shedding their seeds. The open cones resemble a group of thick, irregularly rounded shields held at a center point, with gaps between shields.

Features: Baldcypress can live over a thousand years. The wood is highly prized for many commercial uses. Lumber from mature trees is rot- and termite-resistant, a feature not found in lumber from young trees. The unique root system, which forms above ground cone-shaped "knees," makes this tree extremely strong against the wind. Baldcypress and its rare almost identical twin Pondcypress can best be differentiated by their leaves in summer.

Natural Range: Baldcypress naturally occurs in and around water, and its range wraps around the lowlands of the southern coastal states and extends up the Mississippi River valley. This tree also has been successfully planted on a wide variety of sites throughout the eastern United States and even some parts of Canada.

BASSWOOD

American Basswood, *Tilia americana*
American Linden

American Basswood is a large tree that can reach 100 feet (30.5 m) in height and 2 to 4 feet (.6 to 1.2 m) in diameter at breast height. It can be identified as one of the basswoods by looking at the soft, light gray-brown bark that is moderately thin with long, shallow, parallel, V-shaped fissures and flat-topped ridges with gently rounded edges. Overall, the bark looks as if it has been compressed against the tree, molding both the ridges and fissures into a pattern that does not have rough edges. Young bark, high in the tree, is smooth and light gray. Large trees often have sprouts growing around the base.

American Basswood (page 67) can be distinguished from the very similar Mountain Basswood (page 67) by looking at the leaves, when present. The alternate, heart-shaped leaves are 5 to 6 inches (127 to 152.4 mm) long, with offset bases that are larger on one side than the other and pointed tips. The leaf is light green with a hairless, smooth bottom surface, whereas the lower surface of a Mountain Basswood leaf is white and woolly. Sometimes, even late in winter, clusters of pea-size berries can be seen dangling like spread fingers from the center of small, elbow-shaped wings that are attached to twigs.

Features: American Basswood is highly prized by bees, which use its flower pollen for making honey. The soft, lightweight wood has many commercial uses, and its soft texture and fine finishing characteristics make it highly prized by wood-carvers.

Natural Range: American Basswood is usually found growing in bottomlands, lower slopes, and valleys. Its range is from North Carolina and Tennessee northward to the Canadian border.

Mountain Basswood, *Tilia heterophylla*
White Basswood

Mountain Basswood is a large tree that can reach 100 feet (30.5 m) in height and 2 to 4 feet (.6 to 1.2 m) in diameter at breast height at maturity. It can be identified as one of the basswoods by looking at the soft, light gray-brown bark that is moderately thin with long, shallow, parallel, V-shaped fissures and flat-topped ridges with gently rounded edges. Overall, the bark looks as if it has been compressed against the tree, molding both the ridges and fissures into a pattern that does not have rough edges. Young bark, high in the tree, is smooth and light gray. Large trees often have sprouts growing around the base.

Mountain Basswood can be distinguished from the very similar American Basswood by looking at the leaves, when present. The leaves (page 67) are 3 ½ to 5 inches (88.9 to 127 mm) long, with bases that have one side higher than the other. The leaf is rounded to an abrupt tip, with a coarse, sharp-toothed margin. The bottom surface is white and woolly, whereas the lower surface of an American Basswood leaf is light green and smooth. Sometimes, even late in winter, clusters of pea-size berries can be seen dangling like spread fingers from the center of small, elbow-shaped wings that are attached to twigs.

Features: Mountain Basswood is highly prized by bees, which use its flower pollen for making honey. The soft, lightweight wood has many commercial uses, and its soft texture and fine finishing characteristics make it highly prized by wood-carvers.

Natural Range: Although it is usually rare wherever it is found, the Mountain Basswood grows throughout the eastern United States.

BEECH

American Beech, *Fagus grandifolia*

American Beech can grow into a large tree, reaching 60 to 80 feet (18.3 to 24.4 m) in height and 2 to 3 feet (.6 to .9 m) in diameter breast height. Its bark remains very thin, hard, smooth-surfaced, and mouse gray no matter how big it grows. It is particular about growing in moist, well-drained areas, including valleys and north-facing lower slopes, where it often grows in pure stands. Because of its dense summer foliage, the area under the tree is usually free of any undergrowth except occasional beech sprouts. Relatively small branches come off the main trunk at right angles. Small branches and twigs have a pronounced zigzag pattern, with a long, slender, needlelike bud and leaf scar at each outside turning point along the twig.

Alternate, simple, lance-shaped leaves (page 68) grow along the stem in two rows that are across from one another like wings on an airplane. They are sharp-tipped, 3 to 5 inches (76.2 to 127 mm) long, and coarsely toothed, with straight veins that stand out on the bottom of the leaf. After turning yellow in the fall, some of the dead leaves may hang on the tree most of the winter. Those that do, soon bleach out to a light tan color. Small trees are especially likely to retain their leaves throughout most of the winter. The tree bears small, triangular nuts.

Features: American Beech is the tree on which people love to carve their names and initials. The wood is close-grained and hard, but it is difficult to dry and machine work. It is one of the finest fuel woods, but its interlocking grain makes it very hard to split. Beechnuts are sweet and nutritious and are eaten by a wide variety of wildlife.

Natural Range: American Beech can be found growing throughout the eastern United States.

BIRCH

Sweet Birch, *Betula lenta*
Black Birch, Cherry Birch

Sweet Birch is a medium to large tree that reaches 50 to 60 feet (15.2 to 18.3 m) in height and 2 to 3 feet (.6 to .9 m) in diameter at breast height. It can be identified by its tight, dark silver-gray to almost black bark, marked with horizontal rows of raised, fine, reddish brown lines one above the other, usually less than ¼ inch (6.4 mm) apart. Occasionally the bark will peel loose horizontally and stand out from the trunk like torn paper. Branches look small for the size of the tree.

Sweet Birch leaves (page 71) are 2 to 4 inches (50.8 to 101.6 mm) long and irregularly double-toothed, with an elongated arrowhead shape. They are smooth on both surfaces, except for fine hairs along the lower-surface veins. Scraping a twig or crushing a leaf will release a strong wintergreen odor.

Features: The wood is used for a wide variety of commercial purposes. When exposed to light, the wood darkens to a deep mahogany color. The sap is extracted for use in products that incorporate wintergreen oil. Many browsing animals eat the buds and twigs.

Natural Range: The range of Sweet Birch extends from southern Maine down the Appalachian Mountains to northern Alabama and Georgia.

Paper Birch, *Betula papyrifera*
White Birch, Canoe Birch, Silver Birch

Paper Birch is a medium-size tree, maturing at 50 to 70 feet (15.3 to 21.3 m) in height and 1 to 2 feet (.3 to .6 m) in diameter at breast height. It is easily identified by its white bark that peels in sheets to the side, revealing a pale yellow lower surface. White Birch often grows in clumps, and from a distance it may be confused with the aspens or Yellow Birch. Closer examination makes the distinction easy, however, because neither aspen nor Yellow Birch bark peels from the trunk this way. The white bark of the trunk has prominent raised horizontal lines, called lenticels, and often has black lines down from either side of its branches, forming what look like black mustaches. On older trees, the bark at the base of the trunk becomes black and furrowed. The narrow, open crown is made up of slender branches that grow from the trunk at right angles and sometimes droop slightly. The reddish brown twigs are usually smooth but are occasionally hairy.

The arrowhead-shaped leaves of Paper Birch (page 72) are alternate, simple, 2 to 4 inches (50.8 to 101.6 mm) long, and 1½ to 2 inches (38.1 to 50.8 mm) wide. The base is rounded and the tip long and slender. The leaf blade is smooth on both surfaces and double-toothed. Two-winged nutlet seeds borne in loose, dangling cones that are 1½ to 2 inches (38.1 to 50.8 mm) long develop in late summer to early fall.

Features: The bark of Paper Birch has been harvested over the centuries by the northern tribes of Native Americans, who built canoes and houses from it and fashioned utensils such as plates, cups, and bowls. Small rolls of bark are often used to start campfires in wet weather, because the bark burns readily even when wet.

Natural Range: Paper Birch grows throughout the Great Lakes states and New England. A variety called Mountain Paper Birch also extends down the Appalachian Mountains through North Carolina and Tennessee.

River Birch, *Betula nigra*
Black Birch, Red Birch, Water Birch

River Birch is a medium-size tree that often grows to heights between 40 and 80 feet (12.2 and 24.4 m) and diameters between 1 and 2 feet (.3 and .6 m) at breast height. It usually develops gently curving trunks covered with very rough, ragged-looking, reddish brown to cinnamon red bark that tries to peel horizontally. Salmon pink to bronze-brown bark that peels loose horizontally in tough, papery layers readily identifies younger trees. The crown often has a helter-skelter look, because it is made up of scattered major branches from which noticeably smaller, slender, zigzag, crooked branches grow out in all directions.

Leaves (page 73) grow two-ranked down the sides of the long, slender twigs in openly alternate fashion. They are 1½ to 3 inches (38.1 to 76.2 mm) long and have a broadly triangular shape with a broad base that roundly tapers to a pointed tip. The leaf edges have both coarse and fine teeth. The top is dull, dark green, and the lower surface is a lighter yellowish green. Veins are more or less evenly spaced as they flare out in almost straight lines from the center vein. In late summer, clusters of two-winged seeds develop in dangling cones that are 1 to 1¼ inches (25.4 to 31.8 mm) long.

Features: River Birch is the most tolerant of the birchs of summer heat, and is common in the southeastern United States for this reason. The wood tends to be knotty and is therefore of limited commercial use, although it is utilized in some furniture because of its lightweight. Its ability to occupy floodplains and along streams and rivers makes the tree valuable for wildlife as cover. The seeds are also eaten by many birds.

Natural Range: It can be found growing from east Texas northeastward up the Mississippi River floodplain through southeastern Iowa. It also ranges eastward through all of the southern states and northward to eastern New York.

Yellow Birch, *Betula alleghaniensis*
Gray Birch, Silver Birch, Swamp Birch

Yellow Birch can be a large tree, with mature heights of 70 to 100 feet (21.3 to 30.5 m) and diameters of 1⅔ to 2½ feet (.5 to .8 m) at breast height. It develops a broad, rounded crown of drooping branches. Side branches are usually noticeably smaller than the trunk. A mild wintergreen odor typically is released when a twig is scraped with a fingernail. Yellow Birch bark is thin, paperlike, and yellowish gray, peeling from the side in thin curls. The trunk is marked with randomly placed fine horizontal lines, called lenticels. As the tree gets larger, the bark on the lower trunk becomes reddish brown and divides into scaly plates that are separated by shallow fissures. Yellow Birch trees sometimes look as though they are standing on three or more legs because they grew over stumps or logs that have rotted away, leaving only exposed roots holding the trunk in the air.

Leaves (page 58) are alternate, simple, and 2 to 4 inches (50.8 to 101.6 mm) long, often growing in slightly offset pairs. The blade is dull green and broadly oval, with fine, sharp-pointed teeth. Brown, egg-shaped cones are ¾ to 1¼ inch (19.1 to 31.8 mm) long and stand upright along the stem. They look as if they have fluffed themselves up against the cold, slowly falling apart over the winter.

Features: Yellow Birch is an important lumber tree. The wood is one of the major sources for wood alcohol. Larger mammals such as deer and moose browse on the leaves and twigs, and the buds are also eaten by wildlife.

Natural Range: Yellow Birch is native to the Great Lakes states and New England. It also follows the highest elevations of the Appalachian Mountains to northeast Georgia and the Cumberland Plateau to southern Tennessee.

BOXELDER

Boxelder, *Acer negundo*
Ashleaf Maple, Boxelder Maple, Manitoba Maple, California Boxelder, Western Boxelder

Boxelder is a small to medium-size tree that usually reaches mature heights of 30 to 60 feet (9.1 to 18.3 m) and diameters up to 2 ½ feet (.8 m) at breast height. It is rounded and often forked, with many opposite branches, twigs, and buds. The wood is very brittle, frequently leaving the trees with broken tops. Long, purplish green, slender sprouts that are often covered with a white dust may grow out in clumps from the trunk and the sides of major limbs. The bark is soft and forms small, block- or diamond-shaped ridges separated by deep, narrow fissures. Rubbing off the surface bark will reveal a creamy to tan inner bark. The texture and inner color resemble ash bark, but the typical presence of long, blue-green twigs distinguishes the Boxelder from the ashes. Bud scars on the twigs are opposite one another and almost meet each other at raised ridge junction points on the top and bottom of the twigs.

The opposite, compound leaves (page 39) are 5 to 15 inches (127 to 381 mm) long, with three to five leaflets (rarely seven) growing along the sides and end of the leaf stalk. The leaflets are 2 to 4 inches (50.8 to 101.6 mm) long and coarsely toothed. There may be one or more lobes with varying shapes. Some lobes look like a thumb jutting out to the side.

Features: Boxelder is often planted as a fast-growing shade tree. It is often a poor choice, because in addition to being short-lived and brittle, it serves as a host to boxelder bugs, which love to crawl into houses for the winter. Boxelder is a good choice for shelterbelt and windbreak plantings, as it can survive poor planting conditions in a wide variety of harsh environments. While it can be found in poorer soils, it prefers moist soils and is often common in swamps or along river banks. The wood is of little commercial value because it is very weak and brittle.

Natural Range: Boxelder can be found growing throughout the United States and Canada.

BUCKEYE

Yellow Buckeye, *Aesculus octandra*
Big Buckeye, Buckeye, Sweet Buckeye

Yellow Buckeye is the largest of the buckeyes, reaching over 90 feet (27.4 m) in height and 3 feet (.9m) in diameter at breast height. It can be difficult to identify in the winter because of its bark variability. Young bark is thin, smooth, and gray, with occasional prominent bumps. As the tree grows and ages, the bark darkens and in some cases turns a tan to yellow-brown. It remains thin but becomes flaky, with irregularly sized, disklike flakes that crack loose from any or sometimes all edges on older trees. Large, old trees often develop an intricate molded face pattern in the bark. Buckeye limbs grow opposite from one another and at right angles from the main stem. They remain unusually small in relation to the size of the trunk.

Yellow Buckeye leaves (page 41) are opposite and compound, with five leaflets spreading out in a fan shape from a central point at the end of a long stalk. They are usually 4 to 6 inches (101.6 to 152.4 mm) long, with broad, pointed tips and tapered bases, and are dark green above and yellowish green below. Margins may have both fine and coarse teeth. Leaves are odorless when crushed; if the crushed leaf or stem releases a rank odor, the tree is an Ohio Buckeye. Searching the ground for the dark brown, nutlike fruit with a light tan eye or encased in a thick, smooth husk will often positively identify the tree as a buckeye.

Features: Yellow Buckeye fruit is poisonous to humans. The tree was given its common name by pioneers, who thought the dark brown, shiny fruit looked like the eye of a buck deer. It is occasionally planted as an ornamental tree, even though it is quite messy in the fall.

Natural Range: Yellow Buckeye prefers to grow in rich, deep, moist soils like those found in river bottoms or deep mountain valleys. It is found from central Ohio and southwestern Pennsylvania southwest down the Appalachian Mountains to northern Georgia and Alabama.

BUTTERNUT

Butternut, *Juglans cinerea*
Oilnut, White Walnut

Butternut is an uncommon, small to medium-size tree that often reaches 60 feet (18.3 m) in height and 1 to 2 feet (.3 to .6 m) in diameter at breast height. The bark of young trees is a light ash gray, with thin, dark streaks that will eventually form valleys in the bark pattern. As the tree ages, the bark becomes quite thick and rugged, developing long, wide, wandering ridges and deep, wide valleys. The ridge tops usually remain wide, flat, and light ash gray in color. The rugged valleys often become wider than the ridges and remain a dark charcoal gray. The resulting effect looks as if an inexperienced painter half tried to whitewash the tree. Butternut twigs are thick and have chambered pith. Each leaf scar along the twigs has a row of hairs along the top of the bud.

Leaves (page 96) are 15 to 30 inches (381 to 762 mm) long, with eleven to seventeen leaflets that are 2 to 4 inches (50.8 to 101.6 mm) long. Leaflets are sharply toothed, with pointed tips and broadly pointed to rounded bases. The upper surface is yellowish green and smooth; the lower surface is paler and covered with hairs. The nutlike fruit is 1½ to 2½ inches (38.1 to 63.5 mm) long and covered with a densely hairy, sticky husk. The meat contained in the roughly grooved shell is sweet but quite oily. It is edible if found before it becomes rancid.

Features: Several Butternut varieties have been developed for nut production. In New England, the tree's nuts are popular for making maple-butternut candy. Pioneers made a yellow dye from the fruit husks and obtained sugar from the sap. Native Americans also used the inner bark of the roots to make medicines.

Natural Range: Butternut is usually found growing along streams or in deep, well-drained soils. Its range is from the Great Lake states and southern Maine southward along the Appalachian Mountains to northern Georgia and westward to the Dakotas and Arkansas.

CATALPA

Northern Catalpa, *Catalpa speciosa*
Candle-Tree, Catawba, Cigartree, Hardy Catalpa, Indian Bean,
Indian Cigartree, Shawnee-Wood, Western Catalpa, Western Catawba

Northern Catalpa is a medium to large tree, often growing 40 to 75 feet (12.2 to 23 m) tall and 1 to 2 feet (.3 to .6 m) in diameter at breast height. The tree's often-twisted trunk usually has flat, scaly bark that is rough and reddish brown to smoke-gray in color. Limbs are arched, twisted, and crooked. Twigs at the ends of these limbs are encircled by sets of large, two-paired and three-whorled leaf scars.

The leaves (page 29) are heart-shaped, 6 to 12 inches (152.4 to 304.8 mm) long, and 4 to 8 inches (101.6 to 203.2 mm) wide. They grow in pairs of two or whorls of three, with two large leaves and one smaller leaf attached to the twig at a common junction point. The tip tapers uniformly to a point. The crushed leaf is odorless.

In late spring, trees bloom with orchidlike flowers that are white with purple spots. They soon develop into clusters of sticklike fruit pods that average ⅝ inch (15.9 mm) in diameter and 9 to 20 inches (228.6 to 508 mm) long. The pods usually hang in pairs and may be either straight or twisted. Close observation will reveal a smooth attachment end and a rounded, dull to medium-sharp tip. The fruit has long rectangular seeds, and blunt-tipped wings at each end of the fruit body. (The wings must be dry to properly discern the shape.)

Features: Spring clusters of flowers are very showy, attracting humans, insects, and hummingbirds. The often-present catalpa sphinx caterpillars, commonly called catalpa worms, make excellent fishing bait when cut in half and turned wrong side out on the hook.

Natural Range: The natural range for Northern Catalpa once centered in west Tennessee, where it was fairly restricted, but because of its popularity, it has been planted and grown throughout the eastern United States.

Southern Catalpa, *Catalpa bignonioides*
*Candle-Tree, Catawba, Cigartree, Hardy Catalpa, Indian Bean,
Indian Cigartree, Shawnee-Wood, Western Catalpa, Western Catawba*

Southern Catalpa is a small to medium-size tree that seldom grows over 40 feet (12.2 m) tall and 1⅔ feet (.5 m) in diameter at breast height. The tree's short, often twisted trunk usually has smoke gray bark, with rough, flat plates and shallow fissures. Twigs at the ends of the widely spaced, arched, twisted, and crooked limbs are encircled by sets of large, two-paired and three-whorled leaf scars.

Southern Catalpa (page 29) leaves are heart-shaped, 5 to 10 inches (127 to 254 mm) long, and almost as wide. They grow in pairs of two or whorls of three, with two large leaves and one smaller leaf attached to the twig at a common junction point. The leaf edges round down to an abrupt long, slender tip. The leaf usually releases a foul odor when crushed.

In late spring, Southern Catalpa trees bloom with white, irislike flowers. By midsummer, the slender, sticklike fruit pods develop and then hang on the tree most of the winter. The pods are pencil-thin, growing less than ⅜ inch (9.5 mm) in diameter and 9 to 20 inches (228.6 to 508 mm) long. They are usually straight, hanging down in sets of two per stalk. There is a round ring around the top of the pod at the point where it joins with the stalk, reminiscent of a tiny wedding band on a very long finger. The tip of the pod is pinpoint sharp and will draw blood if pressed too hard. The pods are filled with long, tapered, slender-tipped, winged seeds. (The seeds must be dry to see the effect.)

Features: Southern Catalpa is a popular shade tree. The often-present catalpa sphinx caterpillars, commonly called catalpa worms, make excellent fishing bait.

Natural Range: Southern Catalpa's natural range probably centered in southern Mississippi, but because of its popularity as a shade tree, it has been planted and grown throughout the eastern United States.

CHERRY

Black Cherry, *Prunus serotina*
Wild Black Cherry, Rum Cherry, Cabinet Cherry

Black Cherry is a medium to large tree, averaging 80 feet (24.4 m) tall and 2 feet (.6 m) in diameter at breast height at maturity. It develops a long, limb-free trunk in forest settings and can be identified by its dark silver-gray to black bark that looks as flaky as if someone had glued large, black cornflakes up and down its trunk. Small trunks, limbs, and twigs have series of random fine, white lines, called lenticels, across them. Scratched twigs or crushed leaves have a distinctively pungent odor. Branches are often quite small and short relative to the trunk size.

   The alternate, simple leaves (page 59) are 2 to 6 inches (50.8 to 152.4 mm) long. The leaf blade is oval to spear-tip-shaped, with a wedge-shaped or rounded base and pointed tip. It is shiny on top and paler below, with rusty-colored hairs along the bottom midvein and fine, incurved teeth along the edges. Small glands may protrude from either side of the petiole just below the blade. Clusters of sour-tasting cherries develop in late summer.

Features: Black Cherry wood is highly prized for furniture and veneer. It is pink when fresh, but when exposed to light, it soon darkens into a rich red patina. All types of wildlife eat the prolific annual crops of cherries; people also occasionally use the cherries for making wine and jelly. In spring, this tree is a favorite home for eastern tent caterpillars.

Natural Range: Black Cherry can be found growing throughout the eastern United States.

Carolina Cherrylaurel, *Prunus caroliniana*
Laurel Cherry, Carolina Cherry, Wild Orange

Carolina Cherrylaurel is a small tree that seldom grows larger than 40 feet (12.2 m) in height and ⅚ foot (.3 m) in diameter at breast height. It is a southern, semievergreen tree that can be found growing singly or in clumps or thickets. When leaves are present, the quickest way to identify this tree is by picking and crushing them. If a distinct cherry fragrance is released, the tree is a Carolina Cherrylaurel. Other identifying characteristics are smooth, gray bark with long, raised lines, called lenticels, on small trunks or smooth to sometimes thin, square-mosaic–patterned bark on larger trunks. Parallel rows of holes drilled by sapsuckers may be present.

Leaves (page 46) are alternate, simple, and 2 to 4 ½ inches (50.8 to 114.3 mm) long by ¾ to 1½ inches (19.1 to 38.1 mm) wide. They are a long, oval-tapered shape, pointed at both ends. The thick-textured, glossy leaf blades are dark green on top and pale green beneath. Edges are usually smooth but may have an occasional tooth. The petiole is orange to red in color. Small clusters of stalked, round fruit often remain hanging on the tree all winter.

Features: Carolina Cherrylaurel is often used as an ornamental for hedges or a small feature tree. The leaves contain prussic acid, which may be fatal to livestock if eaten in large quantities. Birds eat the fruit.

Natural Range: Carolina Cherrylaurel can be found growing throughout the South, from North Carolina to Texas. The heaviest concentrations are along the coastal plain, where it often forms dense thickets.

CHINABERRY

Chinaberry, *Melia azedarach*
China Tree, Pride of China, Pride of India

Chinaberry is an exotic tree that has become naturalized throughout the South. It is a short-lived, small to medium-size tree that usually reaches 30 to 50 feet (9.1 to 15.2 m) in height and 1 to 1½ feet (.3 to .46 m) in diameter at breast height. The trunk is usually short and often multiple-stemmed. The gray bark is thin, with variably long, flat-topped plates lying on a thin, flat base. Chinaberry wood is very brittle and breaks easily, leaving the crown filled with broken limbs and stubs. The remaining limbs are long, slender, and upward-pointing. Twigs are stout and have continuous, white-colored center pith.

Leaves (page 105) are alternate, doubly compound, and 10 to 20 inches (254 to 508 mm) long, with ragged-looking, arrowhead-shaped leaflets that are 1½ to 2½ inches (38.1 to 63.5 mm) long. Leaflets have long tips and coarsely toothed edges that are sometimes lobed. Both the top and bottom surfaces are smooth. In the spring, clusters of purple flowers bloom. Clusters of yellow fruit that are ¼ inch (6.4 mm) in diameter and poisonous develop later in the summer and remain on the tree into the fall. The foliage has a bitter taste and strong odor when crushed. The foliage is not poisonous, but remember the fruit is.

Features: Originally planted as an ornamental, Chinaberry escaped cultivation and is now considered by many to be a noxious weed.

Natural Range: Chinaberry trees were brought to the southern United States from the Himalayan region of Asia and were widely planted throughout the region. They have become naturalized in most of the southern states.

COTTONWOOD

Eastern Cottonwood, *Populus deltoides*
Alamo, Carolina Poplar, Eastern Poplar, Necklace Poplar,
Southern Cottonwood

Eastern Cottonwood is a large tree with the ability to reach mature sizes of over 100 feet (30.5 m) in height and 4 feet (1.2 m) in diameter at breast height. Young trees often look as if their trunks are stuck full of arrows, with short, slender branches growing at right angles to the trunk. As the tree matures, the lower branches drop off, leaving a tall single trunk topped by a crown of strong, well-spaced branches. The bark on young trees is yellowish green to gray, thin, and smooth. It gets thicker as the trees mature, eventually becoming thick and rough, with deep crevices and rounded ridges. Occasionally portions of the bark have light silver-gray, chalk–dust-like coloring in their crevices. Looking up into large trees reveals a change in bark character from rounded ridges to shiny, flat-topped plates. Farther out the limbs, the bark changes yet again to a smooth light gray.

Leaves (page 69) are triangular and 3 to 5 inches (76.2 to 127 mm) long. The base of the leaf blade is almost straight across. Teeth along leaf edges vary from medium coarse to rounded. The petiole is flat-sided and very flexible. Trees flower and bear fruit in early spring. The small, round seedpods hang in clusters that eventually crack open, releasing individual cottonlike seeds that float on the wind for some distance before reaching the ground. The resemblance of these seeds to cotton gives the tree its name.

Features: Eastern Cottonwood is commercially harvested and used for many products, including lumber, veneer, and pulpwood. It is also widely planted as a shade tree.

Natural Range: Eastern Cottonwood grows west of the Appalachian Mountains from Canada to the Gulf of Mexico. In the south, it expands eastward to the Carolinas and Georgia.

DOGWOOD

Flowering Dogwood, *Cornus florida*
Dogwood, Eastern Flowering Dogwood

Flowering Dogwood is a small tree seldom reaching more than 20 feet (6.1 m) in height and ½ foot (.2 m) in diameter, with a rather flat, spreading crown and short, often crooked trunk. It is an understory tree, most often found growing under taller hardwoods. The bark is tan to dark brown and broken up into small, four-sided, scaly blocks. During the winter, the branch tips usually have large, flat-topped, rounded flower bracts, modified leaves that show an X when looked at from the end.

Leaves (page 30) are opposite, simple, and shaped like a fat football. The veins make pronounced sweeping, upward curves from the centerline of the leaf to the smooth outside edges. The tree blooms in spring, with small flowers surrounded by four large, white, petal-like bracts that form what looks like large, white flowers. In the fall, the leaves turn burnt red and the tree has clusters of red berries.

Features: Flowering Dogwood is one of the most popular flowering trees in the southern United States, with many varieties cultivated and sold. The berries are an important source of food for many birds. Wild dogwoods have become scarce in many forests as a result of a deadly anthracnose fungus called dogwood discula. The wood of Flowering Dogwood is white, heavy, fine-grained, and very hard. At one time it was commercially harvested for products with requirements for smoothness and toughness, such as weaving shuttles, spools, pulleys, and mallet heads. Pioneers used the wood to make kitchen utensils, gristmill cog teeth, and horse collars.

Natural Range: Flowering Dogwood grows throughout the eastern United States and is commonly planted as an urban tree.

ELM

American Elm, *Ulmus americana*
Florida Elm, Soft Elm, Water Elm, White Elm

American Elm is a large tree reaching 100 feet (30.5 m) in height and 4 feet (1.2 m) in diameter at breast height. The overall shape of the tree and its twig pattern can identify American Elm. The tree usually forks sharply into two or more trunks. The resulting multiple trunks branch out and arch gracefully away from one another, with ever finer branching patterns up to the very fine-textured, upturned branch tips. The crown thus looks like a loosely arranged bunch of long-stemmed dried flowers in a tall vase. The bark pattern is a series of long, narrow, parallel, rough, flat-topped ridges separated by equally narrow, sometimes deep valleys. Cutting a cross section of the dark brown to gray-black bark will reveal distinct parallel, cream-white lines in the reddish brown inner bark.

Leaves (page 73) are 3 to 5 inches (76.2 to 127 mm) long, alternate, simple, double-toothed, lopsided at the base, and pointed at the tip. The upper surface is usually smooth but may occasionally be quite rough. The bottom of the leaf blade is smooth.

Features: Even though Dutch elm disease decimated many trees in the past and remains a periodic threat, natural survivors and the development of resistant varieties are helping the American Elm make a comeback as a premium urban shade tree. Its wood is moderately heavy, hard, and stiff, with an interlocking grain that makes it hard to split. American Elm flowers in early spring, causing allergic reactions in many people. The fruit that develops is a small, winged, saucer-shaped disk. Because of its small size, it usually goes unnoticed.

Natural Range: American Elm can be found growing throughout the eastern United States.

Cedar Elm, *Ulmus crassifolia*
Basket Elm, Red Elm, Southern Rock Elm

Cedar Elm is a medium to large tree that reaches heights of 80 to 100 feet (24.4 to 30.5 m) and averages 2 to 3 feet (.6 to .9 m) in diameter at breast height. Its base is unique, with a shape that may be swollen and deeply fluted, square, triangular, or a combination of the three, but it is seldom simply round. A long, narrow crown of heavy, crooked limbs sits at the top of the long, clear trunk. The purplish gray bark is flat and fairly thin, breaking into rectangular, flat-topped plates that are separated by thin, shallow cracks. The bark often curls outward slightly at the top and bottom of each plate. Smaller Cedar Elm twigs are often corky, with two long ridges of cork that usually are not taller than ¼ inch (6.4 mm).

The small, boat-shaped, double-toothed leaves (page 74) are 1 to 2 inches (25.4 to 50.8 mm) long and ½ to 1 inch (12.7 to 25.4 mm) wide, with a very rough upper surface and parallel, straight veins. The base is lopsided, and the tip is broadly pointed or rounded. The petiole is ¼ inch (6.4 mm) long and covered with woolly hairs. Most elms flower in the spring, but Cedar Elm flowers and fruits in the fall. The fruit is flat and disk-shaped, with hairy wings and a deep notch at the tip.

Features: Cedar Elm is common in Oklahoma and Texas, where it is often planted as a shade or street tree. The wood has great shock resistance and strength. It is harvested and commercially marketed as Rock Elm. Squirrels feed on the buds, and several species of birds eat the fall seeds. Cedar Elm blooms about the same time as ragweed and has been known to complicate or worsen allergies and late-summer hay fever.

Natural Range: Cedar Elm can be found from southwest Tennessee and northwestern Mississippi through southern Arkansas and western Louisiana to western Texas. It prefers to grow along major river drainages but can also be found on drier sites.

September Elm, *Ulmus serotina*

September Elm grows 40 to 60 feet (12.2 to 18.3 m) tall and 2 to 3 feet (.6 to .9 m) in diameter at breast height. It is a graceful tree that forks low to the ground and flares outward, with several trunks dividing into long, slender branches ending in very long, fine twigs, resembling a dried flower arrangement in a tall, slender vase. The twigs often have small, corky wings growing on two, three, or even four sides. The grayish brown to reddish brown bark is rough, with long, narrow, interlocking bark plates separated by equally rough, shallow valleys of about the same width and length.

Alternate, simple leaves (page 74) grow in two ranks on opposite sides of the branch and are 2 to 3 ½ inches (50.8 to 88.9 mm) long and half as wide. The leaf has a lopsided base, broadly tapered sharp tip, and doubly toothed edges with sharp teeth. The top of the blade is dark green and smooth; the lower surface has very fine hairs along the central vein that can sometimes be seen only by using magnification. Veins are straight and pale white. The tree flowers and fruits in late fall. The flattened seed is surrounded by a wafer-thin, circular wing, with a deep notch in the tip. It is about ½ inch (12.7 mm) long and covered with fine hairs.

Features: September Elm is used as a shade or street tree. In areas where the tree is common, it is harvested and marketed as elm. Although it looks similar to American Elm, its fall flowering and corky branches can identify it as September Elm.

Natural Range: September Elm is a relatively rare tree with a very limited range, growing in spotty fashion throughout Kentucky, Tennessee, northern Mississippi, Alabama, and Georgia. It also grows westward into Arkansas.

Slippery Elm, *Ulmus rubra*
Gray Elm, Moose Elm, Red Elm, Soft Elm

Slippery Elm is a medium-size tree seldom growing larger than 70 feet (21.3 m) in mature height, with diameters ranging from 1 to 2 ½ feet (.3 to .8 m) at breast height. In an open situation, it usually develops a large top filled with long, tapered branches that end with very thin, upward-turned twigs. From a distance, the crown's shape is reminiscent of two open hands touching at the wrist and then spreading away from one another with upreaching, slightly cupped fingers. Young twigs and buds are covered with reddish hair. Chewing the twig will release a lightly flavored, gluelike, slippery sap, which gives the tree its name.

Slippery Elm's thin bark ranges in color from light silver-gray to reddish brown. Bark texture is a matrix of thin, wide, tight, flat-topped, rough-edged ridges with rounded ends divided by shallow, irregularly shaped valleys. Although recognizable curved, interlocking bark ridge lines occasionally run up the tree, the individual bark plates often look more as if they are a plastered collection rather than divided from one another by a system of ridges and valleys. Slicing through the bark at a gradual angle will usually expose thin layers of white inner bark divided by the thicker reddish brown bark, as usually found in the elms.

Slippery Elm leaves (page 75) are double-toothed, 4 to 7 inches (101.6 to 177.8 mm) long and 2 to 3 inches (50.8 to 76.2 mm) wide, and fairly oval. The leaf has a pointed tip and lopsided base. The upper surface is dull, dark green, and sandpaper-rough; the bottom is very hairy and also feels somewhat rough. Fruit is a very small, flat, papery, circular, winged disk that is borne in the spring.

Features: Slippery Elm is harvested and marketed commercially for wood products as soft elm, but its claim to fame is in the pharmaceutical trade, where its bark and sap are used in making various natural remedies. Although not typically planted as an ornamental tree, it often provides shade by growing up in adjoining fencerows.

Natural Range: Slippery Elm grows throughout the eastern United States, from Maine to North Dakota in the north and Florida to Texas in the south.

Winged Elm, *Ulmus alata*
Cork Elm, Wahoo

Winged Elm is a small to medium-size tree that is usually less than 50 feet (15.2 m) tall and 1½ feet (.5 m) in diameter. It has a wide, oval to round top made up of long, slender, wandering branches, many of which are winged with wide, corky ridges that are usually present along two sides, making Winged Elm easy to identify. The bark of Winged Elm is light gray, thin, and very irregularly shaped, with rough but more or less flat plates and shallow fissures. When shaved or blazed, the bark shows thin bands of dark and buff white inner layers.

Leaves (page 75) are 1½ to 3 inches (38.1 to 76.2 mm) long and 1 to 1½ inches (25.4 to 38.1 mm) wide, with evenly spaced, coarse teeth divided by fine teeth between. One side of the leaf is wider than the other, as though the yellow center vein is slightly off to one side of the rounded base. The upper surface may be either smooth or rough; the lower surface is smooth.

Features: This small tree is sometimes used as a yard tree, especially if it was on the property before the house was built. It is too small to be commercially important in the lumber market. The wood grain is interlocking and difficult to split. At one time the inner bark was soaked and woven into rope. Dutch elm disease, which has been deadly to most elms, does not usually affect Winged Elm.

Natural Range: Winged Elm is common throughout most of the south, from southern Virginia to Texas.

FIR

Balsam Fir, *Abies balsamea*
Canada Balsam, Eastern Fir

Balsam Fir is a small to medium-size evergreen tree that reaches mature sizes of 40 to 60 feet (12.2 to 18.3 m) in height and 1 to 1½ feet (.3 to .5 m) in diameter at breast height. The trunk grows straight up, often bristling with very short branches from the ground to the top, forming a narrow, spire-shaped tree. Balsam Fir can be distinguished from its closely related Appalachian neighbor Fraser Fir *(Abies fraseri)* by looking for the aromatic pitch pocket blisters that develop on the light gray bark of the trunk, which only Balsam Fir has. In addition, the bracts of the cones on Fraser Fir project beyond the scales, whereas on the Balsam Fir they do not.

The short, awl-shaped needles (page 16) with a series of light stripes along the bottom that make the needles look silver-gray from below also identify the Fraser Fir. When present, small cones stand erect on the branches the first year. After shedding their seeds, these cones slowly fall apart in place, leaving spikelike stems sticking up.

Features: Balsam Fir is commercially important within its range. It is harvested and marketed for pulpwood and light frame construction, and it is one of the most popular Christmas tree species. Wildlife rely on this tree for protection from the weather and eat its seeds and twigs. Its presence adds beauty to the landscape.

Natural Range: Balsam Fir is a Canadian tree that grows southward to the northern edges of Minnesota, Pennsylvania, and Iowa and eastward throughout New England.

GINKGO

Ginkgo, *Ginkgo biloba*
Maidenhair-Tree

Ginkgo trees are native to China but are also widely planted throughout the eastern United States, where they do especially well in the middle and southern states. Young Ginkgo trees are pyramidal in shape, with a central trunk surrounded by a whorled cluster of sharply upturned branches. Mature trees become more wide-spreading. The light gray bark has a ridge-and-valley texture, with flat-topped ridges that are crooked, rounded on the edges, and broken into various lengths by surrounding shallow, rough-textured valleys. Small branches and twigs have well-spaced, right-angled, stubby twig spurs that are ½ to 1 inch (12.7 to 25.4 mm) long, with clustered leaf scars on the end of each stub.

Alternate, simple, triangular leaves (page 81) that are 2 to 3 inches (50.8 to 76.2 mm) long and wide grow in clusters from short spurs. The leaf flares out in a fan shape from a narrow beginning point at the petiole to a wide end that is entire or sometimes divided into two or more wide, blunt teeth. Fruit is a silver-white seed covered by a tan to orange pulpy skin. The fruit is about 1 inch (25.4 mm) long and releases a very dis-agreeable odor when mashed.

Features: Ginkgo trees are often called living fossils, because they are one of the oldest tree species still living on earth. Given time and good grow-ing conditions, they can grow into massively impressive trees, with lime green leaves that turn bright yellow in the fall. The seeds are roasted and eaten as a delicacy in China and Japan.

Natural Range: This tree is thought to be native to China, but this is speculation, because to date no naturally planted Ginkgo has been found growing in the wild. It has been cultivated for centuries in eastern Asia and Japan and is now widely planted in the eastern United States.

HACKBERRY-SUGARBERRY

Hackberry, *Celtis occidentalis*
Common Hackberry, Nettle-Tree, Hoop Ash, Beaverwood, Northern Hackberry, American Hackberry

Hackberry is a medium to large tree that reaches 60 feet (18.3 m) in height and 1½ to 2 feet (.5 to .6 m) in diameter at breast height. It is often found growing in fencerows and almost pure stands in shallow, limestone-based soils. Like the beech, it has smooth, mouse gray bark, but individual and clusters of warty growths protrude from the smooth surface at random places. These protrusions are usually ¼ to ⅓ inch (6.4 to 8.5 mm) tall and twisted-looking. Warts can range from ¼-inch (6.4 mm)-long singles to rows along the smooth bark. A second identifying feature is the tangles of twisted twigs that often develop at the ends of branches and resemble birds' nests.

Hackberry leaves (page 60) are light green, 2 to 4 inches (50.8 to 101.6 mm) long, and 1 to 2 inches (25.4 to 50.8 mm) wide. The leaf has a lopsided base, tapered tip, and three major veins spreading from the stalk and sweeping up through the blade, with the center vein running straight to the leaf tip. The edges of the blade have fine, forward-facing teeth. Hackberry has small orange-red to blue-black drupes (identical to a berry except with a hard surface). These are very sweet and juicy and are favored by wildlife.

Hackberry and its close relative Sugarberry are so similar that in areas where their ranges overlap, they are hard to tell apart with any certainty in either summer or winter. Some taxonomists solve the problem by labeling the tree in question as being Hackberry-Sugarberry. A simple rule of thumb for winter identification might be that if the tree is covered with warts and growing from Tennessee northward, it is probably Hackberry; if it is relatively smooth and growing south of Tennessee, it is more likely Sugarberry. They also can sometimes be differentiated by the leaves; see the description under Sugarberry (page 47) .

Features: Hackberry wood is soft and featureless. It is used in manufacturing as a utility wood and sometimes as a veneer on which wood grains are
(continues on page 204)

printed. Birds eat the berries. Although seldom planted for the purpose, Hackberry is often found growing as a shade tree in urban environments.

Natural Range: Hackberry grows from the southern regions of the Great Lakes states southward through Tennessee.

Sugarberry, *Celtis laevigata*
Southern Hackberry, Sugar Hackberry, Texas Sugarberry, Lowland Hackberry

Sugarberry is a medium to large tree growing to 80 feet (24.4 m) in height and 1½ feet (.5 m) in diameter at breast height. It has a rounded top, smooth mouse gray bark, and branches that hang down at the tips. Warty growths may be found scattered on the trunks of older trees, but they are not usually as prominent or numerous as those found on the closely related Hackberry. The trunk usually is gently curved rather than straight and is often forked low to the ground. Lichens form both dark and light patches on the bark surface, creating mosaiclike patterns that add texture to the tree. The twigs at the branch ends are often tangled like frizzed hair.

Because Sugarberry and Hackberry trees are so closely related, they are difficult to tell apart with any degree of certainty in the winter. See the description of Hackberry for some clues to their identity.

Sugarberry also can be distinguished from Hackberry by looking at the leaves (page 47). Sugarberry leaves grow in two rows and are alternate, 2 to 4 inches (50.8 to 101.6 mm) long, simple, and arrowhead-shaped, with long, slender tips and off-sided round bases. Edges may be smooth or have a few scattered teeth. Three major leaf veins flare out from the petiole at the base of the leaf. Fruit is small orange-red to blue-black drupe.

Features: The sweet Sugarberry fruit is eaten by a wide variety of birds and small animals. The wood does not have the typical lumber grain, so it is used commercially in places where it will not be seen and occasionally in making plywood panels with imprinted wood grains.

Natural Range: Sugarberry commonly grows as far north as Indiana and southeastern Virginia. To the west, it extends through much of Oklahoma and Texas. With the exception of the deepest swamps in Louisiana, it can also be found growing all along the Gulf coast and throughout Florida.

HEMLOCK

Carolina Hemlock, *Tsuga caroliniana*

Carolina Hemlock is a small to medium-size, graceful-looking, evergreen tree that seldom grows over 60 feet (18.3 m) in height or 2 feet (.6 m) in diameter at breast height. The lower limbs usually droop down toward the ground in flat, layered fashion and flare upward at the tips. The bark is rough and fibrous, showing many shades of brown. The needles (page 17) present the best positive identification. They are ½ to 1 inch (12.7 to 25.4 mm) long, flat, and blunt-tipped, with two parallel light blue stripes along the bottom from end to end. For all practical purposes, Carolina and Eastern Hemlock look the same except for size and the way the needles grow from the twig. Unlike Eastern Hemlock needles (page 18), which grow in two parallel rows, the needles of the Carolina Hemlock point out in all directions.

Features: Carolina Hemlock grows well in the deep shade of other trees. This slow-growing tree may take 250 to 300 years to reach maturity and may live more than 800 years. The wood is used commercially, but possibly its most important purpose is protecting and cooling forest streams. Within its range, Carolina Hemlock is a popular urban tree.

Natural Range: Carolina Hemlock is almost always found in moist, well-drained areas, such as lower drainages and north-facing slopes. It has a scattered but limited natural range that includes the highlands of southwest Virginia, northeast Tennessee, western North Carolina, western South Carolina, and the tip of northwest Georgia.

Eastern Hemlock, *Tsuga canadensis*
Canada Hemlock, Hemlock Spruce

Eastern Hemlock is a medium to large, graceful evergreen tree that reaches mature heights of 60 to 80 feet (18.3 to 24.4 m) and diameters of 2 to 3 feet (.6 to .9 m) at breast height. It usually retains its branches halfway down the trunk and sometimes all the way to the ground. The lower limbs typically droop down toward the ground in flat, layered fashion and flare upward at the tips. The bark is rough and fibrous, showing many shades of brown. The needles (page 18) present the best positive identification. They are ½ to ¾ inch (12.7 to 19.1 mm) long, flat, and blunt-tipped, with two parallel light blue stripes along the bottom from end to end; but unlike Carolina Hemlock needles (page 17), they grow opposite and in flattened parallel rows.

Features: Unlike most other trees, Eastern Hemlock grows well in the deep shade of other trees. This slow-growing tree may take 250 to 300 years to reach maturity and may live more than 800 years. The wood is used commercially, but possibly its most important purpose is protecting and cooling forest streams. Eastern Hemlock is a popular urban tree. A serious non-native insect pest, the hemlock wooly adelgid (*Adelges tsugae*), threatens to eradicate entire stands of this tree from the eastern forests of the United States.

Natural Range: Eastern Hemlock is almost always found growing in cool, moist, well-drained valleys, north-facing slopes, and along waterways. Its natural range is from New England and the northern Great Lakes states down the Appalachian Mountains to north Alabama.

HICKORY

PECAN-HICKORY GROUP

Bitternut Hickory, *Carya cordiformis*
Bitternut, Swamp Hickory

Bitternut Hickory is a large tree that can reach 100 feet (30.5 m) in height and 2 to 3 feet (.6 to .9 m) in diameter at breast height. It commonly prunes itself quickly, developing a long, limb-free bowl up to a large, rounded crown. The bark on young trees is smooth, gradually becoming tight and interlacing as the tree gets larger. The thin bark usually changes from a network of interlaced ridges to long, flat ridges and shallow fissures toward the crown. The bark continues to become smoother and smoother going toward the end of each limb.

Leaves (page 96) are 6 to 10 inches (152.4 to 254 mm) long, with seven to eleven narrow leaflets that are 4 to 6 inches (101.6 to 152.4 mm) long. Leaflets are bright green on top and pale below, with light fuzz on the lower surface. Leaflet margins are fine to coarse-toothed. In all seasons, the buds at the branch tips are a bright sulfur yellow. Each nut is encased in an almost round husk that has four ridges above the middle and is sprinkled with tiny yellow scales.

Features: Bitternut Hickory nuts are so bitter that almost nothing will eat them. They are all but ignored even by squirrels as long as there is anything else available to eat. The wood is used commercially in manufacturing products that require tough, resilient wood. It is also the choice wood for smoking meats. Pioneers extracted oil from the nuts for oil lamps. This tree has found some use as an urban tree by default, because it withstood the rigors of house construction on wooded lots, but it is seldom if ever planted for this purpose.

Natural Range: Bitternut Hickory grows throughout the eastern United States, with the exception of the New England states and the northern portions of the Great Lakes states.

Pecan, *Carya illinoensis*
Sweet Pecan

Mature Pecan trees growing in forested situations develop into very large, straight-stemmed trees with heights exceeding 170 feet (51.8 m) and occasionally reaching over 5⅚ feet (1.8 m) in diameter at breast height. Cultivated varieties usually fork 4 to 8 feet (1.2 to 2.4 m) above the ground and are shorter with broad-spreading crowns. The bark on young trees is light brown to silver-gray, thin, split into short, narrow, flaky plates divided by intersecting shallow, narrow fissures. As the tree ages, the bark becomes rougher, forming long, narrow, thick, loosely attached plates divided by deep, narrow cracks. Many old trees have smoother patches of bark on the trunk, with unusual sets of straight indentations across the surface. These indented lines often intersect one another at angles, forming triangular shapes. They are so straight they look man-made. The strong limbs are well spaced and tend to come off the trunk at right angles.

Leaves (page 97) are 12 to 20 inches (304.8 to 508 mm) long, with eleven to seventeen short-stalked, curved, sharply pointed leaflets that are 3 to 7 inches (76.2 to 177.8 mm) long. The alternate, dark yellow-green leaves cluster at branch ends. Fine teeth rim the edges of leaflets.

Nuts are oval, husk-covered, and borne in clusters. The thin husk covering the nut has four tall wings running from base to tip.

Features: Pioneers found the Pecan throughout the South and harvested the prized nuts for food whenever they could beat wildlife to them. There are now many cultivars bred for better-tasting, larger nuts for home and commercial use. The wood is marketed as pecan or hickory and is used for furniture, flooring, and fuel. Pecans develop both male and female flowers on the same tree. Different varieties that match one tree's male flowering dates to another tree's female flowering dates are planted together to make sure pollination takes place and nuts are produced.

Natural Range: Pecan prefers growing in rich, moist river bottoms, and its major natural range is the lower Mississippi River valley. Within this region, the range reaches from southern Illinois to east Texas. Commercially developed cultivars are grown throughout the South.

Water Hickory, *Carya aquatica*
Swamp Hickory, Bitter Pecan

Water Hickory is a large tree that may reach 110 feet (33.5 m) tall and 3 feet (.9 m) in diameter at breast height. A long, narrow crown of slender to moderately thick, upward-reaching branches tops the tall, straight trunk. The bark is thin, with flat-topped plates separated by thin, shallow cracks, and ranges in color from light tan to dark brown, with a purple-red tinge on the plates. As the tree ages, the flat bark plates break loose from the trunk and hang in long, loose scales.

The alternate, compound leaves (page 101) are 9 to 15 inches (228.6 to 381 mm) long, with seven to thirteen dark green, narrow, sickle-shaped leaflets growing from short stalks. The leaflets are 2 to 5 inches (50.8 to 127 mm) long and ½ to 1½ inches (12.7 to 38.1 mm) wide, with curved tips and finely toothed edges. Both the base and tip of each narrow leaflet are pointed. Leaflets are lopsided and crescent-shaped, with one side of the blade wider than the other. The nuts are flat and oval, covered with rough, pebbly husks.

Features: Water Hickory is an important part of the wetland forests that clean our water. It is seldom used commercially, because its wood is inferior to that of the other hickories, but locally it is a favorite firewood. The nuts are eaten by wildlife if nothing else is available. Both the Latin and common name refer to Water Hickory's ability to live and grow in wet sites.

Natural Range: Water Hickory is most often found growing in swamps and coastal plains. It can be found growing in the Atlantic and Gulf coastal plains from southeastern Virginia to eastern Texas. Its range also reaches northward up the Mississippi River floodplain to southern Illinois and south to the Florida Everglades.

TRUE HICKORY GROUP

Mockernut Hickory, *Carya tomentosa*
Bullnut, Hognut, Mockernut, White Hickory, Whiteheart Hickory

Mockernut Hickory occasionally reaches 100 feet (30.5 m) in height and 3 feet (.9 m) in diameter at breast height, but it usually ranges from 50 to 80 feet (15.2 to 24.4 m) in height and 1½ to 2 feet (.5 to .6 m) in diameter. The trunk is free of branches before spreading into a thick, oblong crown. The major branches reach sharply upward while supporting drooping side branches. The mouse gray bark is very tight, with interlocking flat to gently rounded ridges laced together over shallow crevices that make the trunk look as if it is wrapped in a tight net. Limbs and young trees have smooth bark broken only by wide lines that eventually define the interlacing bark. Beginning on each side of many limbs, a slightly raised, deeply indented bark crease flows down the side of the tree. These closed liplike creases are key characteristics that can be used for distinguishing Mockernut Hickory from other hickories. The two prominent crease lines protrude out from the bark, are rounded on both edges, and crease deeper than the rest of the bark. The overall effect makes the tree look as though it is frowning severely.

Alternate, compound leaves (page 97) are 8 to 12 inches (203.2 to 304.8 mm) long, with five to nine (usually seven) deep green to yellow-green leaflets. Leaflet edges are fine- to coarse-toothed. The leaflets release a strong odor when crushed. Both the leaflet bottoms and complete leaf stalk (petiole and rachis) are covered with fuzz, and large buds are hairy. Nuts with very small fruit cavities are clothed in thick, round to pear-shaped husks that have indented seams.

Features: Mockernut Hickory is tough and can take abuse, making it excellent for products such as tool handles. It is also used in steam bending because of its flexibility. The nuts are a favorite of squirrels.

Natural Range: Mockernut Hickory grows from Massachusetts and New York west to southern Michigan and northern Illinois, south to eastern Texas, and east to northern Florida.

Pignut Hickory, *Carya glabra*
Broom Hickory, Coast Pignut Hickory, Pignut, Smoothbark Hickory, Swamp Hickory

Pignut Hickory often grows to heights of 80 to 90 feet (24.4 to 27.4 m) and occasionally reaches 120 feet (36.6 m) tall, with mature diameters at breast height of 3 to 4 feet (.9 to 1.2 m). This large tree develops a tall, oval crown of relatively short branches, the lowest of which droop toward the ground. The gray bark is smooth and tight on young trees, slowly becoming scaly but not shaggy as the tree ages. The bark often looks looser than it really is. The ridges are vertical, occasionally interlacing with one another but generally remaining separated by shallow, flat-bottomed furrows that run up and down the tree. Brown twigs are slender, smooth, and hairless.

Pignut Hickory leaves (page 98) are alternate, compound, and 6 to 14 inches (152.4 to 355.6 mm) long, with five to seven leaflets (usually five) that are dark green above and pale below. Leaflets are smooth on both top and bottom, with sharp-toothed edges. The entire leaf stalk, both petiole and rachis, is smooth and hairless. The terminal buds are blunt, starting out shiny green or brown and later shedding the outer scales to expose hairy inner buds. The nuts are one of the quickest ways to identify Pignut Hickory. They are 1 inch (25.4 mm) long and encased in pear-shaped husks that crack about halfway open at maturity. Many of these nuts remain on the ground at the base of the tree for months, because they are so bitter they are not a highly preferred food for wildlife.

Features: Pignut Hickory is commercially harvested and sold as hickory. It is used for many products that require tough, flexible wood, such as tool handles. Pignut Hickory often becomes an important shade tree by default in wooded urban settings because of its ability to live through the abuses of house construction. It is seldom if ever planted for this purpose, however, as its nut crops make it a rather messy yard tree.

Natural Range: Pignut Hickory can be found growing on a wide variety of sites throughout the eastern United States.

Red Hickory, *Carya glabra* var. *odorata*
Carolina Red Hickory, Oval Pignut Hickory, Sweet Pignut Hickory

Red Hickory can become a large mature tree that may reach 80 to 100 feet (24.4 to 30.5 m) in height and 2 to 3 feet (.6 to .9 m) in diameter at breast height. The trunk is usually long and limb-free before holding a crown filled with well-spaced, strong limbs. The bark has grayish black cracks and silver-gray ridge tops. Red Hickory bark is very rough, with a pattern that looks as if it once was woven together but weathered and broke apart long ago. It has short, rough, thin, wavy ridges and valleys that do not connect together uniformly. Breaking off the surface bark will reveal a brown brick-colored inner bark.

The alternate, compound leaves (page 99) of Red Hickory are 6 to 14 inches (152.4 to 355.6 mm) long, with seven (occasionally five) lance-shaped leaflets per leaf. The leaflets are 5 to 7 inches (127 to 177.8 mm) long and 1 to 2 inches (25.4 to 50.8 mm) wide, with the upper five leaflets being about the same size. The blades are dark yellow-green and smooth on top, and paler with tufts of hair along the veins on the bottom surface. Edges are finely toothed. The leaf stalk parts, both petiole and rachis, are usually slender and smooth. Terminal buds begin smooth and glossy but soon shed their covering scales, revealing fuzzy buds that are ½ inch (12.7 mm) long and remain exposed for the rest of the winter. The nuts are 1 inch (25.4 mm) long, thin-walled, and round to egg-shaped. The shell readily splits all the way to the base of the nut.

Features: There are several named varieties of Red Hickory. One, Carolina Red Hickory (*C. ovalis* var. *hirsute*), is restricted to the mountains of North Carolina. It has pubescent leaflets and leaf stalks and oval hickory nuts. Red Hickory is commercially harvested and marketed as hickory. The nuts provide food for wildlife.

Natural Range: Red Hickory can be found growing on upland sites from central Iowa through New York in the north to middle Mississippi through Georgia in the south. It is not found on the coastal plain.

Shagbark Hickory, *Carya ovata*
Scalybark Hickory, Upland Hickory

Shagbark Hickory is a medium to large tree reaching 60 to 80 feet (18.3 to 24.4 m) in height and 1 to 3 feet (.3 to .9 m) in diameter at breast height. It has mouse gray, silver-mottled, hard, almost shiny bark that peels up from the bottom in long, thin, overlapping strips and hangs down over the trunk in loose layers. These strips are tough as armor, making them difficult to break off even though with some effort they can be peeled from the tree. The trunk is usually long and free of limbs up to an oblong-shaped crown of relatively short, crooked limbs. This long, narrow crown is consistent whether the tree is grown in a forest situation or in the open. The small, brown twigs are smooth to slightly hairy, and each ends with a large, brown, hairy bud.

Shagbark Hickory leaves (page 100) are alternate, compound, and 8 to 14 inches (203.2 to 355.6 mm) long, with five to seven leaflets (usually five) that are dark yellow-green above and pale and sometimes downy below, with finely toothed edges. The leaf stalk, both petiole and rachis, may be either smooth or hairy. The hickory nut is covered with a yellow-brown to nearly black, four-ribbed husk that is 1¼ to 1½ inches (31.8 to 38.1 mm) long and ¼ to ½ inch (6.4 to 12.7 mm) thick, smooth, and nearly round. This husk splits all the way to its slightly flattened base, releasing a light tan, slightly flattened nut that is ridged on four sides and has needle-sharp tips on each end.

Features: Shagbark Hickory draws attention to itself with its long, narrow, peeling bark scales. The wood is tough and resilient, making it suitable for products that must withstand impact or need to be steamed and bent to form. Many animals eat the large crops of nuts produced annually. Southern Shagbark Hickory and Shellbark Hickory are quite similar to Shagbark Hickory; see their descriptions for comparison (pages 224, 226).

Natural Range: Shagbark Hickory usually prefers to occupy dry sites. It is evenly distributed throughout the eastern United States.

Southern Shagbark Hickory, *Carya carolinae-septentrionalis*
Shagbark Hickory

Southern Shagbark Hickory is a medium-size tree often reaching 50 to 70 feet (15.2 to 21.3 m) in height and 1 to 2 feet (.3 to .6 m) in diameter at breast height. The iron gray, thin, hard bark plates are usually wide and shaggy, peeling from both top and bottom, but they also may be long and narrow, curling up from the base. The bark surface is often covered with light silver-gray or gray-green splotches. In a forested environment, the crooked limbs turn sharply upward and form a narrow crown; when grown in the open, the crown spreads out, taking a broad, rounded form.

Alternate, compound leaves (page 101) are 6 to 10 inches (152.4 to 254 mm) long and have five sharply toothed leaflets per leaf. The slender, spear-shaped leaflets are 4 to 7 inches (101.6 to 177.8 mm) long and one-fourth as wide. The teeth along the edges are noticeably forward-facing. The tip of each leaflet tapers to a long point. The buds are small and glossy brown to almost black in color. The nuts are 1 to 1¼ inches (25.4 to 31.8 mm) long and attached to the ends of slender twigs. When ripe, the husk cracks all the way to the base in four pieces, releasing a light tan, slightly flat, four-sided, prominently ridged nut that has a sharp-pointed tip.

Features: Southern Shagbark Hickory is premium firewood, with exceptionally high Btu heat values. The wood is tough and resilient, making it good for manufacturing products that need to withstand impact or be steam-bent into form. Squirrels and other wildlife feed on the sweet nuts. In areas where the two species grow together, Southern Shagbark Hickory is often misidentified as Shagbark Hickory. Southern Shagbark Hickory has smaller, less hairy leaves than the Shagbark Hickory. The fruit of Southern Shagbark Hickory is also smaller and has thinner husks. Finally, Southern Shagbark Hickory's twig buds are covered with shiny black scales.

Natural Range: Southern Shagbark Hickory is often found growing in shallow, limestone-based soils and on high, dry ridges. Its range is from northeastern Mississippi and east Tennessee east through the piedmont and foothills of the Appalachian highlands of Georgia, South Carolina, and North Carolina.

Shellbark Hickory, *Carya laciniosa*
Kingnut Hickory, Bigleaf Shagbark Hickory, Bottom Shellbark Hickory

Shellbark Hickory is a large tree with the potential to reach over 100 feet (30.5 m) in height and 3 feet (.9 m) in diameter at breast height at maturity. The bark of young trees is smooth and mouse gray, but its narrow ridge-and-valley pattern soon starts to become very rough and scruffy-looking. The narrow bark plates often break loose and curl outward at both ends. Some trees even develop sections of long, loose, peeling bark like Shagbark Hickory. Short, stout branches grow at right angles to the trunk beginning about halfway up the tree.

The alternate, compound leaves (page 100) of Shellbark Hickory are the largest of all the hickories, often reaching 24 inches (609.6 mm) in length. They have five to nine noticeable wide leaflets that are 5 to 9 inches (127 to 228.6 mm) long and 3 to 5 inches (76.2 to 127 mm) wide, with smooth upper and hairy lower surfaces. The central stalk may or may not be hairy. These leaf stalks often remain hanging on the tree throughout the winter after the leaflets have fallen. If the buds and twigs can be reached, the exceptionally large terminal buds, ½ to 1 inch (12.7 to 25.4 mm) long, and the large, orange-brown, hairy twigs with short, raised lines called lenticels can be used to make a positive identification. When present, the goose-egg–size nuts are another good way of identifying Shellbark Hickory.

Features: The tough, flexible Shellbark Hickory wood traditionally has been used for tool handles. The nuts are very sweet and nutritious. Shellbark and the Shagbark Hickories are very similar but can usually be differentiated in winter through close observation.

Natural Range: Shellbark Hickory prefers well-drained, damp areas but will grow on drier sites. It is most common in the Ohio Valley but can be found as far north as New York and as far south as Georgia and Alabama.

HOPHORNBEAM

Eastern Hophornbeam, *Ostrya virginiana*
American Hophornbeam, Ironwood

Eastern Hophornbeam is a small tree seldom growing over 50 feet (15.2 m) tall and 12 inches (305 mm) in diameter at breast height. The thin bark is light tan to brown and has a shredded appearance. The surface bark rubs off readily in the hand. Branches are small and usually grow from the trunk at right angles. The ridges and furrows of the bark are very small, lying flat on the surface of the trunk.

Leaves (page 76) are 2 to 5 inches (50.8 to 127 mm) long and generally oblong, with narrowed tips and rounded bases. Margins are sharply toothed with small, fine teeth and sometimes doubly toothed with occasional coarse teeth. The upper surface is dull yellow-green and smooth, and the bottom is pale green and often slightly hairy. In the fall, the leaves turn bright bronze-yellow. Lateral buds are curved and pointed. The pale green, winged fruit hangs in layered clusters and looks a lot like the fruit of the hops plant used in brewing beer.

Features: Eastern Hophornbeam is one of two trees commonly called ironwood, along with hornbeam, because of their tough, dense, split-resistant, hard wood. It has been used for centuries in making mauls and other tools that have to stand up to a lot of punishment. Eastern Hophornbeam is an understory tree that grows in the shade of its hardwood neighbors. It seems to prefer growing in dry, rocky soils.

Natural Range: Eastern Hophornbeam grows from Maine to Minnesota and south to Florida and East Texas.

HORNBEAM

American Hornbeam, *Carpinus caroliniana*
Eastern Hornbeam, Ironwood, Blue Beech

American Hornbeam is a tall shrub to small tree that seldom grows more than 25.4 to 35 feet (7.6 to 10.7 m) in height and ⅔ to 1⅓ feet (.2 to .4 m) in diameter at breast height. It is easy to identify American Hornbeam by looking at the muscular, flexed-biceps shape of the trunk. The bark is thin, smooth, hard, and blue-gray. American Hornbeam is usually found growing in the shade of its neighbors. The muscle-shaped trunk often twists, turns, and hangs the tree's crown of limbs over to one side in an attempt to reach sunlight.

American Hornbeam leaves (page 76) are alternate, simple, and 2 ½ to 5 inches (63.5 to 127 mm) long, with rounded bases and tapered points. The edges are both fine- and coarse-toothed. The top surface is dark green and smooth; the bottom is pale, with fine hairs along the lower veins. Fall fruit is winged nutlets hanging in pairs in loose, drooping clusters that are 3 to 6 inches (76.2 to 152.4 mm) long. The nut is enclosed in the base of a three-lobed, winglike bract.

Features: American Hornbeam seldom grows tall enough in the hardwood forests to reach the sunlight enjoyed by its larger neighbors. The wood is very dense and hard, but the tree's small size limits its use to such things as mallets and tool handles. Wildlife feed on the fruit and browse on the twigs. The roots help stabilize streambanks.

Natural Range: American Hornbeam can be found growing in wet areas and along streams throughout the eastern United States.

HORSECHESTNUT

Horsechestnut, *Aesculus hippocastanum*
Common Horsechestnut, European Horsechestnut

Horsechestnut is a medium-size tree that often reaches mature heights of 50 to 75 feet (15.2 to 22.9 m) and diameters at breast height of 1 ½ to 2 ⅙ feet (.5 to .7 m). It usually forms a wide-spreading crown that is almost as wide as the tree is tall. The gray-brown bark is smooth on young trees but becomes scaly as the tree grows older. The scales often crack loose at the sides and break off, exposing layers of newer bark.

Horsechestnut leaves (page 42) are opposite, compound, and with seven leaflets that are 4 to 10 inches (101.6 to 254 mm) long and 2 to 5 inches (50.8 to 127 mm) wide, spreading out in a fan shape from a central point at the end of the leaf stem. Leaf petiole can be up to 6 inches (152.4 mm) long. Leaflets flare from a narrow base to the widest point halfway to the tip, and then round down to a sudden, abrupt tip. Coarsely toothed leaflets are dark green on both top and bottom. When the large, shiny, almost black, sticky buds can be seen or reached, they are the easiest way to identify Horsechestnut in winter. White flowers grow in clusters on center posts at the ends of the branches. The fruit is a shiny nut with a pale brown eye encased in a pod that is covered with scattered spines.

Features: Horsechestnut is widely planted in open areas as a street or public park tree. It finds limited use as wood-turning stock in making bowls and as carving stock for wood-carvers.

Natural Range: Horsechestnut is native to Europe. It was brought to the eastern United States many years ago and has enjoyed popularity as an urban tree ever since.

JUNIPERS

Eastern Redcedar, *Juniperus virginiana*
Cedar, Red Juniper

Eastern Redcedar is a small to medium-size evergreen tree often maturing at heights of 40 to 60 feet (12.2 to 18.3 m) and 1 ⅙ to 2 feet (.4 to .6 m) in diameter at breast height. It has a thick, conical crown filled with yellow-green to blue-green, prickly, scalelike foliage. The trunk bark is thin silver-brown and peels or shreds off in long, very thin strips. Larger trunks often develop a fluted base. Pricking through the bark to the wood usually releases a distinctive cedar odor. The young tree has small, sharply upturning branches that form a tight, slender cone shape with a pointed top. As the tree matures, the limbs spread somewhat, forming an oval crown of dense foliage. A very old tree develops an irregularly shaped crown.

The leaves of Eastern Redcedar (page 14) have two forms. Juvenile growth is small and needle-shaped; mature leaves form small, overlapping, blue-green scales. Both forms feel prickly to the touch and grow out in several directions rather than in layers. Cedar-apple rust infections often cause hard, golf-ball-size growths on the twigs. Fruit is 3/16 inch (4.8 mm), blue-gray, and has a soft, berrylike structure.

Features: Eastern Redcedar has traditionally been used for aromatic lumber products, such as cedar chests and closet linings. Its oils are also extracted and used in many products. The pink heartwood is of average strength and somewhat brittle, but it is very rot-resistant, so it can be used with good results in situations requiring soil contact. Many species of birds feed on the cedar berries. The birds' digestive juices break down the seeds' hard coating. When the birds eliminate the seeds, they fall to the ground ready to germinate and grow new trees. Eastern Redcedar is not a true cedar; it is actually a member of the juniper genus of trees *(Juniperus)*.

Natural Range: Eastern Redcedar grows throughout the eastern United States.

Southern Redcedar, *Juniperus silicicola*
Coast Juniper, Coast Redcedar, Pencil Cedar, Red Juniper, Sand Cedar

Southern Redcedar is a medium-size evergreen tree maturing at about 50 feet (15.2 m) in height and 2 feet (.6 m) in diameter at breast height. The deep blue-green, scale-type foliage (page 15) is smooth to the touch and forms a dense crown. If the tree's top branches are lost, the side limbs take over, forming an upward-sweeping, bowl-shaped crown that looks like two hands cupped above touching wrists. The thin twigs are covered with scale-type leaves and grow out in all directions. Bark is reddish brown with a silver cast, very thin, and shreds off in long, stringlike strands. Fruit is ³⁄₁₆ inch (4.8 mm), blue-gray, and has a soft, berrylike structure.

Features: In the Deep South, Southern Redcedar is planted as a featured ornamental and in rows to form dense windbreaks. The heartwood is dull red and has a pleasant, distinctive odor that keeps it in demand for closet linings and cedar chests. It is straight-grained but weak and is easily worked with tools. Southern Redcedar was so heavily harvested in the nineteenth century for pencils that it has never recovered as a prominent forest tree. Birds that eat the small berries plant new trees. The bird's digestive system uses the fleshy fruit and also prepares the seed for germination. Planting is accomplished when the seed passes out of the bird's body, drops to the ground, germinates, and sprouts.

Natural Range: Southern Redcedar is most likely to be found growing along the low Atlantic and Gulf coastal plain from North Carolina to Texas.

KENTUCKY COFFEETREE

Kentucky Coffeetree, *Gymnocladus dioicus*

Kentucky Coffeetree is a medium to large tree that can grow more than 70 feet (21.3 m) in height and 2 feet (.6 m) in diameter at breast height. The loose-looking, rough, outward-curling bark that remains very rough along the branches can identify it quickly. The bark pattern is so rough and contorted it looks as though the body of the tree has been suddenly partially deflated, leaving the bark to erupt in all directions as it is pulled closer together from the inside. The branches grow sharply upward before spreading into an oval crown filled with well-spaced, contorted, thick, rough limbs. Cutting through larger twigs will expose the salmon pink center pith.

Leaves (page 106) are 12 to 24 inches (304.8 to 609.6 mm) long, alternate, and doubly compound, with three to eight sets of side stalks. Each of these side stalks has six to fourteen pairs of oval, smooth-edged leaflets that are 1 to 3 inches (25.4 to 76.2 mm) long. The fruit is a large, fleshy pod that is 4 to 7 inches (101.6 to 177.8 mm) long and 1½ to 2 inches (38.1 to 50.8 mm) wide and contains several hard, black, beanlike seeds. Some of the mature reddish brown fruit often hangs on the tree throughout most of the winter, especially during those years when there is a heavy fruit crop.

Features: The origin of common name Kentucky Coffeetree is hidden in history, but there are two popular explanations. The first is that pioneers or possibly Southern Civil War soldiers roasted the beans and ground them as a coffee substitute. The second is that the person naming the tree found it growing in Kentucky and thought the shiny, brown beans in the fleshy pods looked like coffee beans. Whatever the truth, this naturally rare tree has become a very popular ornamental. It prefers growing in deep, well-drained soils.

Natural Range: Kentucky Coffeetree grows from central New York to Nebraska and down the western side of the Appalachian Mountains through Kentucky and Tennessee and westward to Oklahoma.

LOCUST

Black Locust, *Robinia pseudoacacia*
Yellow Locust, Locust

Black Locust is a small to medium-size tree that seldom grows taller than 50 feet (15.2 m) or more than 1⅓ feet (.4 m) in diameter at breast height. The tree is often crooked, with limbs growing from the central stem at sharp upward angles, often parallel to the tree trunk. The light brown to dark silver-gray, ropelike bark becomes very thick, with long, interlocking ridges and deep, narrow fissures. The inner bark is light tan. The quick identifying characteristic is the presence of paired thorns that are ½ to 1 inch (12.7 to 25.4 mm) long along the twigs and young central stems. Often there are also single thorns growing from older trunk bark. Black Locust often forks into two or more parallel trunks with a very narrow crotch between them. It usually develops an open, upright, oval crown.

Black Locust leaves (page 102) are singly compound and 6 to 10 inches (152.4 to 254 mm) long, with seven to nineteen small, thin, oval leaflets attached in pairs down the central leaf stalk. In summer, the flat, beanlike fruit develops, with about seven small beans inside each shell. Shattered pieces of the shells often remain on the tree most of the winter.

Features: Black Locust often grows in thickets, eventually mingling with other hardwood trees. Its hard, strong, rot-resistant wood makes it a favorite for fence posts and other uses that involve ground contact. The wood is extremely durable in a wide variety of conditions. The tree is a nitrogen-fixing plant, putting usable nitrogen in the soil that other plants can take up.

Natural Range: Black Locust is most often found growing in full sunlight in such places as hedgerows and recently disturbed areas. Its original range ran down the Appalachian Mountains from Pennsylvania south to Georgia. Extensive plantings and escapes from cultivation have made this a rather common tree throughout most of the eastern United States.

Honeylocust, *Gleditsia triacanthos*
Sweet-Locust, Thorny-Locust

Honeylocust is a medium to large tree growing to 80 feet (24.4 m) tall and 1½ feet (.5 m) in diameter at breast height. It often forks into two or more trunks joined by sharp, V-shaped crotches. The tree has thin, light to medium brown, flat, edge-peeling bark that resembles dried and curling leather. The quickest identifying characteristic is the prominent presence of long, sharp thorns growing from both the trunk and larger limbs. The thorns on Honeylocust are quite large and long and often have secondary thorns growing at an angle from the base.

Leaves (page 107) may be either compound or doubly compound and are 6 to 8 inches (152.4 to 203.2 mm) long, with small, rounded leaflets. Leaflets are ⅜ to 1¼ inches (9.5 to 31.8 mm) long and have smooth edges. Blades are shiny dark green above and dull yellow-green below. The fruit matures into a long, thin, flat, beanlike shape. They are usually purplish brown, twisted, and 10 to 18 inches (254 to 457.2 mm) long and 1 to 1½ inches (25.4 to 38.1 mm) wide. They may hang on the tree through most of the winter.

Features: Several thornless varieties of Honeylocust have been developed for urban use. The wood is very heavy and durable in contact with soil. The beanlike pods are quite sweet and eaten by many animals. They have also been grown and tested as a source of oil from which to make biofuels.

Natural Range: The natural range for Honeylocust is the central United States. The eastern edge of the range reaches from western Maryland down the western side of the Appalachian Mountains and continues at the same angle to southern Louisiana.

Waterlocust, *Gleditsia aquatica*

Waterlocust is a medium-size tree that can reach 50 to 60 feet (15.2 to 18.3 m) in height and 1 to 2 feet (.3 to .6 m) in diameter at breast height. In open areas, it usually develops stout, crooked limbs that begin low to the ground. In forest situations, it grows straight up with the neighboring trees, forming a long, limb-free trunk and small, rounded crown. Regardless of shape, the trunk and branches are usually well armed with long, slender, sharp thorns that are sometimes forked and may be up to 4 inches (101.6 mm) long. The thin, dull gray to reddish brown bark is broken into flat to lumpy plates divided by shallow, crooked, vertical cracks. Young Waterlocust stems are green, with numerous small, tan bumps and long thorns.

Waterlocust leaves (page 102) are compound and sometimes doubly compound. They are paired on lateral spurs and are 6 to 10 inches (152.4 to 254 mm) long, with twelve to twenty oval, blunt-toothed leaflets that are ½ to 1 inch (12.7 to 25.4 mm) long. The leaflet surfaces are dark green to yellow-green above and lighter below. The short, flat fruit is 1 to 3 inches (25.4 to 76.2 mm) long and 1 inch (25.4 mm) wide, with one to three seeds inside. The pods occasionally hang as singles but are more likely to be found in clusters.

Features: Waterlocust is used locally for custom cabinets and purposes that require a durable wood that can withstand soil contact for long periods of time.

Natural Range: Waterlocust is usually found growing in moist areas, such as frequently flooded swamps and river bottoms. It grows along the Atlantic and Gulf coastal plain from North Carolina to cast Texas. It also extends up thc Mississippi River floodplain to southern Illinois and southwestern Indiana.

MAGNOLIA

Bigleaf Magnolia, *Magnolia macrophylla*
Largeleaf Magnolia, Silverleaf Magnolia

Bigleaf Magnolia is a small deciduous tree, usually less than 40 feet (12.2 m) in height and ⅚ foot (.3 m) in diameter at breast height. It can be identified as a magnolia by its thin, gray, leatherlike bark and upright form. The bark will dent slightly when pressed with a fingernail and recover its original shape when pressure is lifted, giving the illusion of pressing against tightly stretched skin or thick leather. The bark is generally smooth, but it may also have scattered surface bumps and lumps. Branches are randomly scattered, thick, and drooping, with large leaf scars. Light green terminal buds on the stout, yellow-green, and furry twigs are 1½ to 2 inches (38.1 to 50.8 mm) long and covered with furry white hairs.

In the summer, its huge leaves (page 47) easily identify Bigleaf Magnolia. They are the largest leaves of any native North American tree, averaging 20 to 30 inches (508 to 762 mm) long and 12 inches (304.8 mm) wide. The leaf flares out from a narrow, eared base to the widest section just before the blunt, rounded point. The edges are smooth but wave up and down along the length of the leaf. The bottom of the leaf is covered with white hairs. The flowers bloom in midsummer. The creamy white blossoms are often 20 inches (508 mm) across and give off a strong fragrance. After blooming, the goose-egg–shaped, rose-colored fruit develops. At maturity, the fruit splits open vertically at each red berry to allow its release.

Features: Bigleaf Magnolia is too small and rare to be considered commercially important for lumber production. It is sometimes planted as an ornamental.

Natural Range: Bigleaf Magnolia usually grows in damp, loose, well-drained soils like those in coves and lower valleys. It is rare within its range. It can be found scattered throughout the southern United States, with the largest concentrations in and around the Great Smoky Mountains of North Carolina and Tennessee, as well as in Louisiana and Mississippi.

Cucumber Magnolia, *Magnolia acuminata*
Cucumbertree, Mountain Magnolia, Pyramid Magnolia

Cucumber Magnolia is a medium to large tree that often reaches 60 to 90 feet (18.3 to 27.4 m) in height and 2 to 4 feet (.6 to 1.2 m) in diameter at breast height. The flat, tan-gray bark is soft and somewhat flaky. It can be easily dented or flaked away with a fingernail. When surface bark is flaked away, a reddish brown inner bark is exposed. The cracks between the narrow, flat-topped, sharp-edged plates are also narrow. When viewed from a distance, the bark pattern looks as if a series of long, narrow, vertical knife cuts were made parallel to one another on a flat surface. The branches are short, with the lower ones growing from the tree at almost right angles and the upper ones reaching upward. The overall effect is a tall, triangular crown that is broad at the base and narrow at the top. Scratching or breaking a twig will release a spicy, sweet smell.

Large, scattered, yellow-green leaves (page 48) that are lighter beneath are 6 to 10 inches (152.4 to 254 mm) long and broadly spear-shaped, with rounded bases and tapered tips. The bottom of the leaf is usually covered with soft, fine hairs. The petiole is short and thick. The mature fruit is upright, shaped and textured like a small red cucumber, and about 2 inches (50.8 mm) long. The numerous capsules along the sides of the fruit split open vertically and release bright red berries.

Features: Cucumber Magnolias growing in a forested situation are often very tall, with long, cylindrical trunks that are free of lower limbs. The wood is straight-grained and desirable for many lumber products. The tree's fast growth and pleasing shape also make it a popular ornamental. Because of its vigor, it is a favorite rootstock on which many other magnolia varieties are grafted.

Natural Range: Cucumber Magnolia grows naturally from western New York south to northwest Florida and west to Louisiana and Missouri.

Fraser Magnolia, *Magnolia fraseri*
Mountain Magnolia, Earleaf Cucumbertree

Fraser Magnolia is a small mountain tree that reaches mature sizes of 30 to 40 feet (9.1 to 12.2 m) in height and 1 to 1 ½ feet (.3 to .5 m) in diameter at breast height. It can be identified by its thin, tan to dark brown, leatherlike bark and crooked form. The bark will dent slightly when pressed with a fingernail and recover its original shape when pressure is lifted, giving the illusion of pressing against tightly stretched skin or thick leather. The bark of young trees is very thin and smooth, but it eventually cracks into a shallow, intricate mosaic pattern as the tree ages. Moss and lichens often form light gray patches on the bark's surface. The tree may be found with a single trunk or multiple stems sprouting from the ground.

The spear-shaped leaves (page 48) are usually 8 to 18 inches (203.2 to 457.2 mm) long, with two distinctive earlobes at the base and a broadly pointed tip. The blade edges are smooth. The leaves usually drop straight down and remain recognizable throughout most of the winter. Terminal buds are 1 ½ to 2 inches (38.1 to 50.8 mm) long and may have a thin, white bloom over the base purple color.

Features: Fraser Magnolia is used as an ornamental because of its fast growth, interesting leaves, and showy white flowers. The flowers are large, 8 to 10 inches (203.2 to 254 mm). They are cream-colored with 6 to 9 petals that open in spring. It gets its name from the eighteenth-century botanist John Fraser, who discovered the tree and introduced it into Europe.

Natural Range: Fraser Magnolia is most often found growing in sheltered coves, valleys, and waterways in the mountains from West Virginia to Georgia. It is fairly common in the Great Smoky Mountains.

Southern Magnolia, *Magnolia grandiflora*
Evergreen Magnolia, Bull-Bay, Big-Laurel, Large Flower Magnolia

Southern Magnolia is a medium-size tree that can reach 60 to 90 feet (18.3 to 27.4 m) or more in height and 2 to 4 feet (.6 to 1.2 m) in diameter at breast height. Forest-grown trees develop long, limb-free trunks with smooth, leathery, light brown to gray bark that becomes scaly with age.

The tree is easily identified by its thick, leathery, evergreen leaves (page 49). The leaves are 5 to 8 inches (127 to 203.2 mm) long, alternate, and oblong, with edges that curl downward. Upper surfaces are dark glossy green and lower surfaces are pale green with rust-colored hairs. The petiole is thick and covered with rust-colored hairs. The large, showy flowers have broad, white petals and a pleasing fragrance. After flowering, the Southern Magnolia develops distinctive, dull red, hairy, stalked oval seed cones that are 5 to 10 inches (127 to 254 mm) long. The cones split open in a series of vertical slits, exposing and dropping bright red seeds before drying out and falling to the ground below the tree. These seed cones remain identifiable on the ground all winter.

Features: Because it can reproduce and become established in full shade, Southern Magnolia is considered one of the major species of the potential climax forest of the southeastern coastal plain. An open-grown tree forms a very pleasing thick, oval, evergreen shape that makes it popular for featured ornamental planting. Southern Magnolia is the principal commercial source of magnolia lumber. Florists use the thick leaves in flower arrangements.

Natural Range: The native range of Southern Magnolia extends along the coastal plain from southeastern North Carolina to Texas. It has been extensively planted as an ornamental throughout the eastern United States and all over the world.

Sweetbay Magnolia, *Magnolia virginiana*
Laurel Magnolia, Swamp Bay, Swamp Bay Laurel, Swamp Magnolia,
Sweetbay

Sweetbay Magnolia varies from a deciduous to semievergreen shrub in the north to a large evergreen tree in the south, where mature sizes range from 50 to 100 feet (15.2 to 30.5 m) in height and 1 to 3 feet (.3 to .9 m) in diameter at breast height. The bark of Sweetbay Magnolia is smooth, with a corky texture. Pressing the bark with a fingernail will indent it. When the pressure is released, the indention will return to its original shape. Bark color is usually a variety of tans to grays, with numerous silver-gray splotches up and down the trunk. The trunks of larger trees are usually long and limb-free, with gently sweeping curves from the base to the top of the oblong crown.

Leaves (page 49) are alternate but clustered at the branch tips. They are leathery-textured, canoe-shaped, and 3 to 5 inches (76.2 to 127 mm) long and about half as wide. The upper surface is a lustrous, yellow-green, and the lower surface is white. When crushed, the leaf releases a spicy odor. Terminal buds are about ¾ inch (19.1 mm) long and covered with silky, silvery white hairs. Buds along the side branches are the same but smaller in size. Flowers are showy, large and white. The fruit is an egg-shaped aggregate of seed capsules that open to release bright red berries.

Features: Because of its beautiful white-bottomed foliage, large white flowers, and handsome fruit, Sweetbay Magnolia is often used as a featured shrub or tree in urban situations throughout its range. The aromatic wood of the larger trees is sometimes used commercially as a specialty item. Some taxonomists separate out the large Sweetbay Magnolias growing in central Florida as a different variety designated *Magnolia virginiana* var. *australis.*

Natural Range: Sweetbay Magnolia grows in frequently flooded areas along the Atlantic and Gulf coastal plain from Long Island to east Texas and up the Mississippi River bottoms to southern Arkansas and west Tennessee.

Umbrella Magnolia, *Magnolia tripetala*
Elkwood, Umbrella Tree

Umbrella Magnolia is a small tree that usually reaches 30 to 40 feet (9.1 to 12.2 m) in height and 1 foot (.3 m) in diameter at breast height. It can be identified by its thin, gray, leatherlike bark and crooked form. Its bark will dent slightly when pressed with a fingernail and recover its original shape when pressure is lifted, giving the illusion of pressing against tightly stretched skin or thick leather. The bark is smooth and gray, with some pimples usually present. The tree may be single-stemmed, but typically several stems sprout from a common base. Branches in the treetop are widely scattered, forming an open, spreading crown. The twigs at the end of each of these branches are very stout, with swollen areas completely encircled by large leaf scars at the point where last year's new growth began. The bud at the tip of each twig is large, smooth, and purple, with a tip that often curves to the side.

Leaves (page 50) are 10 to 24 inches (254 to 609.6 mm) long and 5 to 10 inches (127 to 254 mm) wide. The tip is pointed, with a slow, rounded taper back to a pointed base. The petiole is short and stout. Edges are smooth but may wave up and down along the length of the leaf. Midsummer-blooming flowers are large, white, and showy, but they give off a fragrance that many find disagreeable. The short-stalked, egg-shaped fruit is rose-colored and matures in the fall, cracking open at many small, vertical slits to release red berries.

Features: Umbrella Magnolia gets its name from the open-umbrella–like positioning of the leaves. It is often used as an ornamental because of its interesting leaves and showy, white flowers. Wildlife feed on the berries.

Natural Range: Umbrella Magnolia can be found growing from southern Pennsylvania and Indiana south to Georgia and Mississippi.

MAPLE

Black Maple, *Acer nigrum*
Black Sugar Maple, Hard Maple, Rock Maple

Black Maple is a medium-size tree often growing to 80 feet (24.4 m) in height and 2 to 2 ½ feet (.6 to .8 m) in diameter at breast height. The tree usually has a short trunk and a large, rounded top filled with long, upward-reaching branches. Twigs and small branches are positioned opposite one another on larger branches. The bark on the trunk gets quite rough with age, often forming long plates that crack and peel from the side. The tops of the bark plates are flat but rugged in appearance. There are few if any true furrows. The plates simply crack apart in thin layers that give the appearance of plates stacked on top of one another rather than being lined up side by side. Bark color is a blend of black, brown, and silver-gray on top and orange-brown beneath the cracking plates. The trunk is often fluted, giving the tree an even rougher look.

Leaves (page 30) are simple and grow opposite one another. They are usually 4 to 5 ½ inches (101.6 to 139.7 mm) long and wide and have three (sometimes five) lobes that droop noticeably, giving them a wilted look. The sinuses are shallow and rounded. The lobes may have a coarse tooth or two before ending in narrow, blunted tips. The upper surface is smooth and dark green; the lower surface is lighter colored and often covered with fine fuzz. The leaf stalk, or petiole, is long and often fuzzy. Often one or sometimes two opposite, long, narrow, spurlike growths called stipules protrude from the petiole's base just before the junction with the twig. Paired fruit have the bodies joined at the stem and flat wings hanging down from each side.

Features: Black Maple is often confused with the very similar Sugar Maple, with which it freely hybridizes. Both are tapped for maple syrup, used as shade trees, and sold in the commercial lumber market as hard maple.

Natural Range: Black Maple grows in the central states between the Great Lakes and Tennessee.

Paperbark Maple, *Acer griseum*

Paperbark Maple is a small tree that seldom reaches over 40 feet (12.2 m) in height and 1⅙ feet (.4 m) in diameter at breast height. It is easily identified by its beautiful bark, which is smooth, hard, and thin, with patches peeling off from the side in shavinglike curls. Bark color varies from cinnamon to many red-brown shades and hues. The rich blend may also include purples and lavenders. Twigs begin exfoliating their bark during their second or third growing season. The peeling process continues until the tree is quite old. Old trees lose much of their tendency to exfoliate bark, but they retain the rich colors. The tree's overall shape varies, but it is usually oval to round.

Each opposite, compound leaf (page 42) is made up of three blue-green leaflets that are 3 to 6 inches (76.2 to 152.4 mm) long by 2 to 2 ½ inches (50.8 to 63.5 mm) wide, attached at a central point on the stalk. The edges are coarsely toothed to lobed. The leaflet bottoms and the leaf stalk, or petiole, are covered with thick mats of white hair.

Features: Its beautiful bark and resistance to pests make Paperbark Maple a favorite featured landscape plant.

Natural Range: Paperbark Maple is an exotic ornamental tree that is native to China. It was introduced into the United States and now can be found in all but the warmest states.

Red Maple, *Acer rubrum*
Scarlet Maple, Swamp Maple, Water Maple, White Maple, Soft Maple

Red Maple is a medium to large tree with the potential to reach 60 to 90 feet (18.3 to 27.4 m) tall and 1 ½ to 2 ½ feet (.5 to .8 m) in diameter at breast height. It is a challenge to identify because its characteristics change as it matures. Red Maple has thin, smooth, light gray bark when it is small. As it gets larger, it develops thicker, grayish brown, flaky bark that is heaviest at the base of the tree and becomes smoother up the trunk. Full-grown trees may have flaky bark all the way up into the limbs. While this bark is in transition and smooth patches of bark are still present, very small pimples can usually be found scattered over the smooth surface. Forked trunks and limbs growing from the trunk usually have sharp V-shaped crotches. Slender young branch tips are often bright red.

Leaves (page 33) are opposite and simple. They are 2 ½ to 4 inches (63.5 to 101.6 mm) in length and width, with wide, pointed, toothed lobes. Usually there are three large lobes and sometimes two smaller ones. The sinuses between lobes form sharp V-shaped notches.

Features: Red Maple is harvested and marketed as soft maple. It also has some value for maple syrup production, but its greatest value is as an urban tree. The fast growth and beautiful fall foliage, combined with ease of variety development and its ability to grow on degraded soils, have pushed Red Maple into urban prominence as a popular shade tree. The fall foliage of native Red Maples varies from bright yellow flecked with dull red to solid red. In the wild, the twigs are a favorite food of white-tailed deer. Named natural varieties include Trident Red Maple (*Acer rubrum* var. *trilobum*) and Drummond Red Maple (*Acer rubrum* var. *drummondi*).

Natural Range: Red Maple is one of the most abundant trees in the forests of the eastern United States. It can be found growing from Florida to Canada.

Silver Maple, *Acer saccharinum*
River Maple, Silverleaf Maple, Swamp Maple, Water Maple, White Maple

Silver Maple is a medium to large tree, maturing at 50 to 80 feet (15.2 to 24.4 m) in height and 2 to 3 feet (.6 to .9 m) in diameter at breast height. It usually forks low to the ground, with two or three trunks supporting an open, spreading crown. Silver Maple is reasonably easy to identify by looking at its sharply forked form; thin, flat, edge-curling bark; widely spaced branches; and large, often exposed roots. The bark is thin and flat, with parallel ridges that break into plates and curl up on all sides, giving the trunk a scruffy, "unshaven look." Fissures between the plates often expose pink inner bark. Upper bark generally becomes smooth on the limbs. Most Silver Maples develop an interesting ring of curled-up bark around the base of the tree about 6 inches (152.4 mm) above the ground. The bark in this area looks almost as if it is erupting away from the tree. This unique pattern can also be seen in the trunk forks, where the bark plates are compressed by the growing tree, causing the exposed edges to jut out in all directions. Large roots can often be seen above the surface of the ground for 3 feet (.9 m) or more from the trunk.

Leaves (page 33) are opposite and 6 to 8 inches (152.4 to 203.2 mm) long, with prominent, pointed, coarse-toothed lobes and narrow, rounded sinuses. The bottom is a silvery color.

Features: Its fast, early growth and graceful shape make this tree a popular ornamental although often over planted due to its weak-wooded tendencies. Silver Maple logs are harvested and sold along with Red Maple as soft maple. Squirrels eat the buds when no other food is available.

Natural Range: Silver Maple can be found growing almost anywhere in the eastern United States. It prefers moist or deep, well-drained soils where it can get sufficient moisture and for that reason is found naturally along streams, creeks, and rivers.

Striped Maple, *Acer pensylvanicum*
Goose Foot Maple, Moosewood, Whistle-Wood

Striped Maple is a small tree that reaches 30 feet (9.1 m) in height and ⅔ foot (.2 m) in diameter. It is usually easily identified by its smooth, green bark, with parallel, long, thin, white to pale blue stripes waving up and down the trunk. Young trees may occasionally be solid deep green to black in color. The bark on larger trees turns brown, but the limbs and twigs retain their green color and stripes. Bright red buds add to the tree's identifying colors.

Leaves (page 34) are 4 to 6 inches (101.6 to 152.4 mm) long and nearly as wide. They are opposite, three-lobed above the center, and finely toothed. The lobes are short, wide, and pointed. The blade is green above, pale below, and smooth on both top and bottom surfaces.

Features: Although it is too small to be used for lumber products, Striped Maple provides browse for many animals and adds beauty to the forest with its unique bark and beautiful yellow fall color.

Natural Range: Striped Maple is an understory tree that is usually found growing in cool, moist, rocky, forested areas. It ranges from the mountains of Georgia, North Carolina, and Tennessee up through New England to Canada. Its best growth is found in the Great Smoky Mountains National Park.

Sugar Maple, *Acer saccharum*
Hard Maple, Rock Maple

Sugar Maple is a medium to large tree that can reach 60 to 100 feet (18.3 and 30.5 m) in height and 3 to 4 feet (.9 to 1.2 m) in diameter at breast height. In the southern parts of its range, solid black, burned-looking areas on the lower parts of the trunk's light gray bark may identify it. The bark often peels in long strips of tight, side-curling ridges that are very tough and hard to break off. Young trees are smooth and gray, but as the tree gets larger, the bark may begin turning black at the base and splitting and curling from the side. Throughout much of its range, parallel rows of holes ¼ inch (6.4 mm) in diameter made by sapsuckers may often be found on the trunk. In the northern regions, the holes made for tapping the sap for maple syrup are larger and lower to the ground. The crown is often thick, with long, slender branches forming a rounded top. Young Sugar Maple trees frequently have heavily pimpled branches and twigs.

Opposite, smooth leaves (page 34) are 3 to 5 inches (76.2 to 127 mm) long and wide, with smooth edges along five main lobes that have pointed tips. There are deep U-shaped sinuses between the lobes. Five main veins originate at the petiole base and spread into the major lobes. Leaves turn a brilliant yellow-bronze color in the fall. Seeds grow in winged sets.

Features: The deep, inviting summer shade the tree provides and its brilliant yellow fall leaf color make the Sugar Maple very popular as a yard tree. Indians learned to make maple sugar and syrup from the sap. Settlers adopted the practice, which continues today as a major industry in the northern states. The wood is in demand for commercial use for products such as flooring, furniture, and veneered paneling.

Natural Range: Sugar Maple is common throughout the northern half of the eastern United States, from northern Georgia, Alabama, and Louisiana up through New England.

MULBERRY

Red Mulberry, *Morus rubra*
Moral

Red Mulberry is a small to medium-size tree that reaches 40 to 70 feet (12.2 to 21.3 m) in height and 1 to 1½ feet (.3 to .5 m) in diameter at breast height. It has a short trunk and long branches that spread out to form a wide, rounded crown. The brown bark is thin, with long, over-lapping, flat-topped, fibrous plates separated by short, narrow cracks that seldom connect with one another. Inner bark is chocolate brown to purple. If a twig is broken, white sap will usually ooze out.

Trees may have leaves (page 87) with no lobes or a mixture of leaves with no lobes, one lobe, or two lobes all growing on the same tree in two rows per branch. The leaves are 4 to 7 inches (101.6 to 177.8 mm) long and 2½ to 5 inches (63.5 to 127 mm) wide. The base of the blade is lop-sided, with one side wider than the other. The tips are long and sharply pointed. The upper surface is rough and the lower surface hairy. Leaf edges coarsely toothed. Mature fruit is long, cylindrical, red to purple berries that are very good to eat.

Features: Red Mulberry fruit is a favorite food of many birds and other wildlife species, which descend on the ripe berries and often completely clean the tree in less than a day. It is occasionally planted as a feature tree to provide food for birds and shade for humans. The wood is in limited supply and usually finds local use for fence posts or crafts. Pegs made from this wood were used in building sailing ships during colonial times.

Natural Range: Red Mulberry is a widely scattered tree that is usually found growing in moist, well-drained areas such as creek banks and cool, moist coves. It grows throughout the eastern United States from the Great Lakes states and Massachusetts southward through east Texas and Florida.

OAK

RED OAK GROUP

Bear Oak, *Quercus ilicifolia*
Scrub Oak

Bear Oak is a small tree that reaches 18 to 40 feet (5.5 to 12.2 m) in height, 5/12 to 7/12 foot (.1 to .2 m) in diameter at breast height and develops a crown that is 20 to 40 feet (6.1 to 12.2 m) wide. This tree's small stature and leaves give the illusion of a huge oak tree that has been shrunk to a miniature size. The tree usually forks low to the ground, with several major limbs growing out in wide, angled forks. The resultant crown is thickly filled with long, knurly branches that reach toward sunlight, with the lower limbs growing parallel to the ground and the rest forming a broad, rounded top. Small, dead limbs are usually present throughout the crown. The trunk bark is smooth to slightly scaly, with widely spaced, short, narrow, cracklike fissures that reveal pink inner bark.

Leaves (page 88) are 2 to 4 inches (50.8 to 101.6 mm) long and 1½ to 3 inches (38.1 to 76.2 mm) wide, with three to seven lobes, which are separated by shallow sinuses and each end with one to three bristled teeth. The end lobe is usually three-toothed. The upper surface of the thick, leathery leaf is dark green. The lower surface is pale green to gray, with dense, woolly fur. The secondary veins are raised on both surfaces. Acorns are about 5/8 inch (15.9 mm) long, and the cap covers up to half of the nut. The cap is covered with soft, fine hairs on both the inner and outer surfaces.

Features: Bear Oak is usually a shrub that becomes established after a hot fire or other disturbance and occupies the site until it is eventually replaced by larger trees. It is too small to be commercially important, but it provides cover for a wide variety of wildlife. The acorns are very bitter and once thought to be eaten only by bears which gave it the name.

Natural Range: Bear Oak is often found growing in pure stands on hot, dry, poor sites. Its range is from southeastern Maine down through Pennsylvania and the uplands of Virginia and West Virginia.

Black Oak, *Quercus velutina*
Quercitron Oak, Yellow Oak, Yellow-Bark Oak

Black Oak is a medium to large tree that can reach over 80 feet (24.4 m) in height and 2 to 4 feet (.6 to 1.2 m) in diameter at breast height. Even in the forest, it usually develops a balanced set of strong-looking limbs in its top. It has a very tough, tight, rough, dark gray to almost black bark, with no silver streaking. The edges of the bark plate are rugged but rounded over, irregularly shaped, and often cracked into small sections. Deep, narrow, equally rough and irregularly shaped vertical furrows separate them. The deep inner bark growing where the bark of the tree touches the wood is bright orange to yellow and tastes very bitter.

The tough leaves (page 88) are quite variable in both size and shape. They are alternate and 4 to 8 inches (101.6 to 203.2 mm) long, with wide or narrow lobes and deep or shallow sinuses. There are usually five to seven bristle-tipped and irregularly bristle-toothed lobes. The top surface is a lustrous, deep green; the lower surface is lighter in color and covered with very small, light yellow, downy hairs that are easier to feel than see. These tiny hairs can be rubbed off easily with the fingers. By late summer, much of this hair may have been rubbed off, leaving small patches—if any—remaining. There are also quite noticeable longer tufts of hair at junction points along the lower center vein. If acorn caps can be found lying around on the ground, the tree can be identified by looking for the fringed edges formed by the loose tips of the scales.

Features: The wood from Black Oak is marketed as red oak and used for many products.

Natural Range: Black Oak reaches its best size growing in deep, fertile soils, but the largest concentrations are often found on drier sites, where it can compete more successfully for sunlight. Its range is from Maine west to Minnesota and south to Texas and Florida.

Blackjack Oak, *Quercus marilandica*
Barren Oak, Black Oak, Jack Oak

Blackjack Oak is a small to medium-size, scruffy-looking tree that grows in dry areas and usually is no larger than 15 to 45 feet (4.6 to 13.7 m) in height and ⅓ to 1 foot (.1 to .3 m) in diameter at breast height. It develops an irregularly shaped, open crown of crooked branches, with some dead twigs. The bark is dark gray to black, with occasional silver flakes on the surface. The plates are relatively short and wide, with very rough, lumpy, broken valleys of approximately the same width and size as the plates. The thick, rough, hard bark resists breaking away from the tree.

The leaves (page 82) are tough and leathery, triangular, and 4 to 8 inches (101.6 to 203.2 mm) long and wide, with three shallow, broad, bristle-tipped lobes near the end and a narrow but rounded base that may have additional small lobes. The leaf stalk, or petiole, and lower surface are covered with dense, brownish or orangish hairs. The veins are raised on both surfaces. There are one to two acorns on a short stalk that have a reddish brown top-shaped cup with hairy scales. The elliptical nut is ½ to ¾ inch (12.7 to 19.1 mm) long, with a stout point.

Features: Blackjack Oak is one of the few red oaks that manufacture and store a substance called tyloses, which seals its vessels and makes the wood watertight. Its small size and knotty wood keep it from being an important source of lumber, but the wood is used for fence posts, wooden water buckets, railroad cross ties, firewood, and charcoal.

Natural Range: Blackjack Oak can be found growing on dry, sandy or clay soils in a range from Iowa east to New Jersey and New York, south to Florida, west to Texas, and north to Nebraska.

Cherrybark Oak, *Quercus pagoda*
Bottomland Red Oak, Elliott Oak, Red Oak, Swamp Spanish Oak, Scalybark Oak

Cherrybark Oak is a large tree with the potential to grow over 130 feet (39.6 m) in height and 4 feet (1.2 m) in diameter at breast height. The tree is tall, gun-barrel straight, and limb-free from the ground to the developed crown high above. The dark gray to black bark with silver flecking is thin but very rough and flaky, with a plate and fissure pattern that is broken up into irregular, short segments. The dark, rough, broken bark sets this tree apart from other bottomland trees.

Leaves (page 89) are alternate, 3 ½ to 12 inches (88.9 to 304.8 mm) long, and 2 ½ to 6 inches (63.5 to 152.4 mm) wide, with five to eleven tapered lobes ending in one to three bristle tips. The lobes are V-shaped, with the upper edge forming a right angle to the central leaf vein. The base of the leaf forms a broad V-shape to the first set of lobes. The top surface is glossy, and the bottom is covered with pale gray fuzz. Secondary veins are raised on both surfaces. There are one to two acorns on a short stalk that have a chestnut-brown cup with hair scales. The usually rounded brown nut is relatively small, with a length of only ⅝ inch (15.9 mm).

Features: A recognized variety of southern red oak, Cherrybark Oak is one of the largest and fastest-growing oaks in the eastern United States. It is commercially marketed as high-quality red oak. The common name came from the bark's resemblance to that of Black Cherry trees. The Latin name denotes the resemblance of the upside-down leaf to the layered roofs of an Asian pagoda.

Natural Range: Cherrybark Oak is most often found growing in fertile, well-drained bottomlands. Except for the state of Florida, it grows in the entire coastal plain and piedmont region from eastern Virginia to east Texas. It also grows up the Mississippi River bottoms through Arkansas and Tennessee to western Kentucky, southern Illinois, and southeastern Indiana. A small, isolated group also grows in east Maryland. It makes its best growth in the lower Mississippi River basin.

Laurel Oak, *Quercus hemisphaerica*
Darlington Oak

Laurel Oak is a semievergreen tree that can reach 80 feet (24.4 m) in height and over 2 ½ feet (.8 m) in diameter at breast height. The tree loses its leaves slowly throughout the winter, and there are almost always at least a few green leaves left on the tree when the new leaves appear in the spring. The bark of the lower trunk becomes rough with age. It is dark brown to almost black in color, with long, broad, flat-topped plates separated by rounded cracks at both ends and divided by narrow furrows. From a distance, the bark looks like the aerial view of a field that has just been dug with a turning plow. This rough bark pattern becomes a little smoother on the upper trunk and along the major limbs. Unlike most of the other oaks, the twigs are easy to break when bent.

Even in the winter, the leaves (page 50) are the quickest way to identify the tree. They are 2 to 4 inches (50.8 to 101.6 mm) long and ½ to 1 inch (12.7 to 25.4 mm) wide. The leaf blade is narrow and long, with a base that may be either rounded or tapered before flaring out gently along the length of the blade and rounding down to a bristle-tipped end. The resultant shape is something like a tapered butter-knife blade. The leaves on young plants may have two or three broad lobes and shallow sinuses. The blade has smooth edges, a dark green upper surface, a pale green lower surface, and a yellow midrib vein. Both surfaces are smooth. The acorn is ½ inch (12.7 mm) long, almost round, and one-fourth enclosed by a saucer-shaped cup. The acorns take two years to mature.

Features: Laurel Oak is often planted as an ornamental tree. The wood is of little commercial importance but is used as firewood. Wildlife feed on the acorns.

Natural Range: Laurel Oak grows naturally along waterways and in bottomlands but also does well when planted in drier soils. It can be found on the coastal plain from southeast Virginia down through Florida to east Texas and up the Mississippi River floodplain to Kentucky.

Northern Red Oak, *Quercus rubra*
Eastern Red Oak, Gray Oak, Mountain Red Oak, Red Oak

Northern Red Oak often grows to be a very large tree, exceeding 100 feet (30.5 m) in height and 2 ½ feet (.8 m) in diameter at breast height. In forest situations, it grows a long, slender trunk topped by a crown filled with strong, well-spread limbs. Large branches have a ring collar pattern of bark around them where they are attached to the tree. The bark of Northern Red Oak is usually dark gray to almost black, but in some parts of the South, it is exceptionally light-colored. The bark is patterned with shallow fissures running up and down the tree between long, wide, slightly concave plates. Looking up into the tree will usually reveal long, wide, silver streaks along the tops of the plates on the trunk and major branches.

Leaves (page 89) are variable. In the eastern part of the range, they are 5 to 8 inches (127 to 203.2 mm) long and 4 to 5 inches (101.6 to127 mm) wide, with rounded sinuses that are usually less than halfway to the midvein and lobes that are symmetrical, coarsely toothed, and pointed forward. In the western part of the range, they are about the same size but tend to be thicker-textured, with a tough, glossy upper surface and widely spread lobes that point in several directions. The sinuses of the western leaves are often deeper than halfway to the central vein. There are one to two acorns without a stalk. A saucer-shaped cup encloses up to one-half of the nut. The oval, brown nut is ⅝ to 1¼ inches (15.9 to 31.8 mm) long, with gray stripes. Reddish brown hairy scales have dark margins.

Features: Because of its large size, fast growth, and high-quality wood, Northern Red Oak is a premium-valued tree for many commercial purposes and is marketed as red oak. It is also quite popular as a fast-growing urban oak tree. Many forms of wildlife eat the acorns.

Natural Range: Northern Red Oak grows throughout all of the eastern United States, with the exception of the southern coastal plain and the deep Louisiana Delta.

Pin Oak, *Quercus palustris*
Spanish Oak, Swamp Oak, Swamp Spanish Oak

Pin Oak is a large bottomland tree that reaches 50 to 130 feet (15.2 to 39.6 m) in height and 1½ to 4 feet (.5 to 1.2 m) in diameter at breast height. Its thick, layered mat of long branches forms a pointed to rounded top and a pronounced drooping base of lower branches that can be used for identification. Each of the branches has short, pinlike side twigs growing out at almost right angles, which in turn often have right-angled side twigs. The overall effect is that of an ancient sailing ship's square-rigger tilted masts. The trunk bark is very thin but hard, with long, slightly raised, flat-topped, gray-brown ridges and wide, shallow, pink to light tan, flat-bottomed valleys of equal width.

The tough leaves (page 90) are 3 to 5 inches (76.2 to 127 mm) long and have five to seven (usually five) prominent, sharply spiked lobes and broad, deep sinuses that reach almost to the central vein. The lower lobes have a tendency to curve back toward the twig, opening up the mouths of the sinuses. The upper surface of the leaf is deep glossy green and smooth, with a raised midvein. The lower surface is pale green and has small tufts of hair along the raised center vein. There are one to two acorns on each stalk, with smooth scales encircling one-quarter of the nut. The nut is rounded, light brown, and often striped. The nut is ⅝ inch long (15.9 mm).

A closely related species named Northern Pin Oak *(Quercus ellipsoidalis)* looks almost identical. If leaves are present, the two species can be distinguished by looking for Pin Oak's raised lower leaf veins, which are absent on Northern Pin Oak leaves.

Features: Pin Oak can tolerate poorly drained soils and intermittent flooding throughout the winter, though not in the late spring and early summer. It can also withstand late-summer drought. These features; combined with its pleasing shape and fast growth, have made Pin Oak a favorite urban tree.

Natural Range: Pin Oak has been extensively planted throughout the eastern United States but grows naturally across the center of the region, from Wisconsin and northern Arkansas to New York and North Carolina. It can also be found growing along the coast to Vermont.

Scarlet Oak, *Quercus coccinea*
Black Oak, Red Oak, Spanish Oak

Scarlet Oak is a medium to large tree that usually reaches 60 to 80 feet (18.3 to 24.4 m) in height and 1½ to 2½ feet (.5 to .8 m) in diameter at breast height. In forest settings, the top is usually rather narrow and irregularly shaped, but in the open, it develops into a shorter tree with a wide, rounded top. The tree is often poorly formed, with dead branches spiking out of the trunk and a swollen, highly figured base. It frequently has long, silver stripes up and down the trunk on top of the bark plates, especially toward the top of the tree. The bark is tight, dark gray, and hard, with shallow ridges running up and down the tree between wide, flat plates. Inner bark is light pink. The sap has a pungent, urinelike odor.

Leaves (page 91) are lustrous, tough, dark green, and 3 to 8 inches (76.2 to 203.2 mm) long, with five to nine long, narrow, toothed, spiked lobes separated by deep, rounded sinuses that extend almost to the leaf midrib. The bottom of the leaf is smooth except for occasional small tufts of hair along the veins. In the fall, the leaves turn burnt to brilliant scarlet red. The acorns have concentric rings circling their tipped ends.

Features: Scarlet Oak is sold as red oak on the commercial market and used in making all kinds of products that feature red oak lumber. Its fast growth and bright fall color make the tree very popular in urban settings.

Natural Range: Scarlet Oak is usually found growing on dry, sandy or rocky soils. Its range extends south from Michigan and Maine to Georgia and Alabama, skirting along the western edge of the coastal plain from North Carolina through the Gulf states.

Shingle Oak, *Quercus imbricaria*
Laurel Oak

Shingle Oak is a medium-size tree that can exceed 65 feet (19.8 m) in height and 1 to 2 feet (.3 to .6 m) in diameter at breast height. Limbs are relatively small for the trunk size, with the lower limbs drooping downward. Multiple sprouts may develop below major limbs that are lost. The trunk bark is medium in thickness, brown to grayish black, and figured, with long, narrow, flat-topped plates divided by equally long, vertical crevices. The bark is very hard and resistant to breaking away from the tree. Picking down through the surface to the inner bark will reveal pink inner bark that is not visible on the surface.

Leaves (page 52) are alternate, 4 to 6 inches (101.6 to 152.4 mm) long, and 1 to 2 inches (25.4 to 50.8 mm) wide. The boat-shaped leaf is proportioned three times as long as it is wide and is widest along the midsection. The upper surface is a lustrous dark green, with a prominent, light-colored central vein that ends in a spike at the end of the leaf. The edges are smooth and wavy, cupping upward. Fine, white hairs cover the bottom surface. Acorns grow singly or in pairs and take two years to mature. Mature acorns are almost round, ⅜ to ¾ inch (9.5 to 19.1 mm) long, and dark brown, with both vertical stripes and concentric circles around the tip. The reddish brown cap covers about half of the acorn.

Features: Shingle Oak received its name from the straight, wide shingles early settlers could split from its wood. Native Americans reportedly used the bark for medicine. Today Shingle Oak is planted as an urban tree and the wood is marketed commercially as red oak. Because of their bitter taste, the acorns are not a preferred wildlife food, but they are eaten when nothing else is available.

Natural Range: Shingle Oak normally grows on deep, well-drained bottomland soils from Iowa south to northern Arkansas, east to western North Carolina, and north to New York, with isolated populations both north and south of its central range.

Shumard Oak, *Quercus shumardii*
Schneck Oak, Shumard Red Oak, Spotted Oak, Southern Red Oak, Swamp Oak, Swamp Red Oak

Shumard Oak is one of the largest of the red oak group, with the potential to reach 150 feet (45.7 m) in height and over 4 feet (1.2 m) in diameter at breast height. In areas where it grows mingled with Northern Red Oak and Black Oak, it can be especially hard to distinguish, because it hybridizes with both freely, developing leaf and bark characteristics that often overlap with those of the other two trees. If the tree is pure Shumard Oak, however, it can be identified by looking at the base of the limbs, where the bark pattern will flow seamlessly from the trunk up through the junction points and out along the bottom of the limbs. The other two oaks have series of raised bark rings circling the limbs at the junction points.

The bark of Shumard Oak varies from gray to brown, with long, narrow, flat-topped plates divided by shallow furrows that are about half the width of the plates. The upper stem and limb bark flattens into wide, shallow plates, with silver streaks along the top. Silver streaking may or may not extend down the tree to the ground. Often the lower bark loses its streaks as it gets older and rougher. The inner bark is rusty orange in color.

Leaves (page 90) are 5 to 7 inches (127 to 177.8 mm) long and 2 ½ to 6 inches (63.5 to 152.4 mm) wide, with seven to nine multiple bristle-tipped lobes that become broadest toward the tip. They are quite variable, with several shapes present on the same tree. In general, the leaves are broad and have lobes that are often off-center from one another. The upper surface is shiny and dark green; the lower surface is duller and has hair tufts along the center vein. Veins are raised on both surfaces. There are one to two acorns on a stalk that have a thick, saucer-shaped cup with blunt scales. The brown, mature nut is ½ to 1 ¼ inches (12.7 to 31.8 mm) long.

Features: Shumard Oak is marketed as high-quality red oak lumber. Its potentially huge size limits its use as an urban tree to large areas.

Natural Range: Shumard Oak grows from North Carolina to Florida and east Texas in the south and up the Mississippi and Ohio River drainages to Indiana.

Southern Red Oak, *Quercus falcata*
Spanish Oak, Water Oak, Red Oak

Southern Red Oak is a medium-size tree usually growing 50 to 80 feet (15.2 to 24.4 m) in height and 1 to 1½ feet (.3 to .5 m) in diameter at breast height. The trunk is typically round and limb-free, with a slight swelling at the base and strong, well-spaced limbs at the top. The bark is very hard and rough, but it is also quite thin, averaging less than ⅜ inch (9.5 mm) thick. Its tight pattern gives the bark the illusion of being compressed and glued to the tree. Bark patterns vary from sets of long, rough-topped ridges and shallow valleys to clusters of what look like plastered, wet cornflakes. The color varies from light gray to almost black. Lichens growing on the bark surface often give the tree a greenish look. The inner bark is various shades of brown, sometimes with cream-colored, short, fine lines and flecks present. Old trees often develop many small twigs along major branches, giving the tree a hairy look.

Leaves (page 91) are alternate and 5 to 7 inches (127 to 177.8 mm) long, with rusty to hairy undersides. There are two distinct leaf shapes. One resembles a turkey foot, with three lobes and two sinuses. The other is five-lobed, with coarse teeth on the lobes. The end lobe is the longest on both shapes. The base of the leaf is rounded, with the stalk in the middle of the U. Each of the lobes is spike-tipped. The acorns have a thin, reddish brown cup with a hairy surface and a sharp, sometimes hairy, tip. The nut is ⅜ to ⅝ inch (9.5 to 15.9 mm) long.

Features: Southern Red Oak is marketed as red oak and used for many wood products. It is seldom planted as a yard tree, but when it is already present on the site, is often left during construction and adopted as a yard tree. Many wildlife species eat the acorns.

Natural Range: Southern Red Oak grows naturally from New Jersey to northern Florida and from Kentucky to eastern Texas, but it is seldom found in the higher elevations of the Appalachian Mountains or the deep swamps of Louisiana.

Texas Red Oak, *Quercus texana*
Nuttall Oak, Red Oak, Red River Oak, Striped Oak

Texas Red Oak is a medium to large tree that grows to 115 feet (35.1 m) in height and 3 feet (.9 m) in diameter at breast height. It has a swollen base and spreading, horizontal to slightly drooping branches. The bark of young trees is light brown, thin, and tight, with slightly raised, wiggle-shaped plates that tend to cup up at the edges and slightly indented furrows of the same color. When sunlight strikes the brown bark plates, they reflect narrow, silver streaks. Older trees growing in wet areas tend to have splotchy gray bark with occasional, zipperlike, vertical bark cracks on their trunks. Branches are noticeably long, straight, and slender, with the lower ones parallel or slightly drooping down toward the ground.

Leaves (page 92) are alternate, 4 to 8 inches (101.6 to 203.2 mm) long, and 2 ¼ to 5 ¼ inches (57.2 to 133.4 mm) wide, with five to eleven lobes and sinuses that are more than halfway to the central vein. Lobes are spiked, with one to three bristle teeth. Lobes along the midsection of the leaf are usually opposite one another. The leaf blade is relatively thin, with a smooth, dark green upper surface and a pale green lower surface. Tufts of orange hair grow on the bottom of the leaf in the vein intersections. Leaves often stay green on the tree until December. Acorns are ¾ to 1 ¼ inches (19.1 to 31.8 mm) long and have distinct dark, vertical stripes from top to bottom.

Features: Texas Red Oak is commercially important in the floodplains of the Mississippi River. It is harvested as red oak. Wildlife use the acorns as a dependable source of food. Because of its good looks and ability to grow quickly in poor soils, it is fast becoming a popular shade tree within its range.

Natural Range: Texas Red Oak grows in the floodplains of the Mississippi River from southern Missouri to the Gulf of Mexico, where its range spreads from east Texas to southwestern Mississippi.

Turkey Oak, *Quercus laevis*
Catesby Oak, Scrub Oak

Turkey Oak is usually a small tree that seldom grows more than 20 to 30 feet (6.1 to 9.1 m) tall and 1 foot (.3 m) in diameter at breast height. The trunk is small and somewhat crooked, quickly developing into an oval crown of short, scattered branches. The overall look of the tree is rugged and somewhat shaggy, even scruffy. The dark gray to almost black bark is very thick and chunky, with short, narrow plates that are almost as thick as they are long or wide. These bark plates are ruggedly rounded over on top and angle down on the sides to form wide fissures that usually bottom out with jagged crack lines. The plates are broken into rectangular shapes at the top and bottom by jagged cross cracks that are almost as deep as the vertical dividing furrows.

The thick, shiny leaves (page 92) are simple, alternate, and 4 to 8 inches (101.6 to 203.2 mm) long, and grow in clusters on the branch tips. Leaves have three to five lobes, with the two lobes next to the leaf tip projecting out at almost right angles to the tip, forming what resembles a turkey's footprint. The sinuses are very deep, and the lobes are spike-tipped, with one to three bristle tips per lobe. The base is sharply angled from the leaf stalk, or petiole, out to the first set of lobes. Veins stand up above the surface on both the top and bottom of the leaf. Occasional tufts of reddish hair can be found along the veins on the bottom. Acorns are 1 inch (25.4 mm) long, egg-shaped, and brown, with scaly, top-shaped caps that are lined with a woolly inner surface.

Features: Turkey Oak is abundant on poorer and drier, sandy soils, where it is often an understory tree. It has little commercial value, but it does its part to stabilize and build up poor soils. Wildlife eat the acorns.

Natural Range: Turkey Oak is limited to the dry, sandy coastal plain from southeastern Virginia throughout Florida and west to southeastern Louisiana.

Water Oak, *Quercus nigra*
Possum Oak, Spotted Oak, Red Oak

Water Oak is a medium to large tree with the capacity to grow over 90 feet (27.4 m) in height and 2 ½ feet (.8 m) in diameter at breast height. It holds its leaves late into the winter, especially in the southern parts of its range, where it may still have green leaves in early spring. Tree form is strong and tall, with a slightly swollen base and a tall, limb-free trunk up to a rounded crown of strong, well-spaced branches. The bark is smooth and brown on young trees but soon turns darker brownish black in color as it develops long, thin, tight plates with both rounded and flat tops that are separated by shallow furrows. The bark pattern is very tight and thin for the size of the tree, becoming smoother toward the upper limbs.

The alternate leaves (page 85) are 2 to 4 inches (50.8 to 101.6 mm) long and 1 to 2 inches (25.4 to 50.8 mm) wide. They are very variable in shape. Some have no lobes, while others on the same tree may have one or two broad lobes toward the wide end, causing the leaves to resemble duck feet. Lobes may or may not be bristle-tipped. All forms have a dull but smooth, dull bluish green upper surface and a paler lower surface that has small tufts of hair in the vein angles. There are one to two acorns on a short stalk that have shallow, hairy cups. The nut is dark brown, almost black, at maturity. The nut is ⅖ to ⅝ inch (10.2 to 15.9 mm) long.

Features: Water Oak is a relatively fast-growing oak that does well on a wide variety of growing sites and is widely planted as a shade or street tree throughout the South. It is a good producer of acorns, with cyclical bumper crops every few years. Many species of wildlife, especially turkey, ducks, and deer, eat the acorns. The wood is commercially harvested and marketed as red oak. It also makes excellent firewood.

Natural Range: Water Oak is often found growing along streams and in damp bottomlands. It grows naturally on the coastal plain from New Jersey to east Texas. The northern limits of the range circles under the Appalachian Mountains and follows the southern edge of Tennessee to the western part of the state, where it expands along the Mississippi River northward to the edge of Kentucky and westward to eastern Oklahoma.

Willow Oak, *Quercus phellos*
Black Oak, Peach Oak, Pin Oak, Swamp Willow Oak

Willow Oak is a medium to large tree that can reach in excess of 80 feet (24.4 m) in height and 2 ½ feet (.8 m) in diameter at breast height. The major limb systems develop long, fine side branches and mats of very long, thin twigs. The bark is dark brown, thin, tight, and hard, with long, shallow valleys running between low, almost flat-topped ridges. The valleys do not have the pink cast of those of Pin Oak. Young trees form a pointed top, with thick, layered, long, slender branches that grow upward at the top and almost straight out at the bottom and middle of the canopy. As the tree ages, the crown tends to flatten out on top, and the lower branches develop a pronounced drooping.

Leaves (page 52) are 2 to 5 inches (50.8 to 127 mm) long and ½ to 1 inch (12.7 to 25.4 mm) wide. They are thick and leathery, with rolled edges and a small spike at the end of each leaf tip. The upper surface is light green; the bottom is a paler green and often covered with fine, gray hairs. There are one to two acorns; almost without a stalk, they do have shallow, saucer-shape cups. The nut turns brown with faint stripes at maturity and is small at ⅜ to ½ inch (9.5 to 12.7 mm) long.

Features: Willow Oak has been widely planted as an ornamental tree. The wood is marketed as low-quality red oak. It is easily distinguished from the other oaks by its long, narrow leaves. Many species of wildlife eat the acorns. It is an especially important source of food for wood ducks and others migrating down the major flyways.

Natural Range: Willow Oak is most often found growing in wetlands and low areas down the Atlantic coast, from New Jersey to South Carolina and west to Texas and Oklahoma, and ranging up the Mississippi River from southern Louisiana and Mississippi to southern Missouri and Kentucky.

WHITE OAK GROUP

Bur Oak, *Quercus macrocarpa*
Mossy-Cup Oak, Blue Oak, Prairie Oak, Mossy-Overcup Oak

Bur Oak is a large tree with the potential to grow over 100 feet (30.5 m) in height and 3 feet (.9 m) in diameter at breast height. Young trees usually have long, slender branches covered on all sides by heavy, corky ridges. Corky branches may be absent in older trees as limbs become thicker. When this is the case, the rounded treetop is filled with massive branches and the trunk bark is deeply fissured. The bark is dark gray-brown, becoming thick and deeply fissured as the tree matures. The ridges and valleys have a sharply cut look, with little rounding over of the edges. The bark pattern is reminiscent of a carved wooden set of rooster's tail feathers.

Leathery leaves (page 82) are 6 to 10 inches (152.4 to 254 mm) long, with narrow bases and broad, rounded, lobed tips. The midsinuses are often so deep that the leaf looks as if it has a narrow waist and wide, rounded end. The shallower sinuses and wide lobes are both rounded in shape. Acorns are borne singly or in clusters of two or three. A very hairy cap covers more than half of the acorn.

Features: Native Americans are reported to have routinely used Bur Oak as a medication for many ailments and a means of burying their dead above the ground. Perhaps because of their size and long life, many Bur Oaks have become historically important in the states where they grow. The common name is derived from the burlike fringe on the acorn cup. Lumber cut from Bur Oak is treated as a white oak and used for many commercial purposes.

Natural Range: Bur Oak grows throughout the Midwest, from Texas to Canada, and east to Tennessee, Kentucky, and Ohio. Some scattered populations may also be found growing in the northeastern states.

Chestnut Oak, *Quercus montana*
Rock Chestnut Oak, Rock Oak, Tanbark Oak

Chestnut Oak is a medium to large tree that can reach 80 feet (24.4 m) in height and over 3 feet (.9 m) in diameter at breast height. It usually develops a wide-spreading, irregularly shaped crown of large limbs. Possibly its most distinguishing characteristic is the deeply fissured, very hard, symmetrical, flat-topped bark that looks like a series of deep, V-shaped valleys that have been carved up and down the tree trunk. These valleys are so deep and wide that people can often place their fingers completely inside the channels. The bark varies from silver-gray to dark-gray to brown.

Leaves (page 77) are simple, alternate, tough-textured, blunt-toothed, and 4 to 8 inches (101.6 to 203.2 mm) long. They flare gently from a narrow, tapered base to a broad, rounded tip. Each leaf has nine to sixteen main pairs of straight veins that end in the center of each tooth. There are no spikes on the teeth. Acorns are large, ¾ to 1½ inches (19.1 to 38.1 mm) long with an oval chestnut brown nut. They are highly sought after by most wildlife and usually do not last long on the ground. The acorn caps left scattered on the ground are deeply rounded and may be ¾ to 1 inch (19.1 to 25.4 mm) wide.

Features: Chestnut Oak is sold as a low-quality white oak on the commercial market. It is used in the manufacture of many products. For many years, it was harvested for its high tannic acid content, which was used in tanning hides. Acorn crops are sporadic, but when they happen, they can be prolific. Many species of wildlife, including squirrels, deer, and wild turkeys, feed on the acorns when they can be found.

Natural Range: Chestnut Oak can be found growing on dry, rocky sites such as upper slopes and ridgetops from New England and Michigan southward to Georgia and northern Alabama.

Chinkapin Oak, *Quercus muehlenbergii*
Rock Oak, Yellow Chestnut Oak, Yellow Oak

Chinkapin Oak is a medium to large tree usually maturing from 45 to 100 feet (13.7 to 30.5 m) in height and 1½ to 3 feet (.5 to .9 m) in diameter. The bark is light gray to dirty light brown, thin, and quite flaky. Vigorously rubbing back and forth across the bark grain will cause a shower of various size pieces of bark that have broken free. The exposed inner bark is a medium brown. Typically the trunk is relatively short and the crown makes up the majority of the tree's total height. The limbs usually fork sharply upward and then spread out to form an open, rounded crown.

Leaves (page 78) are 2 to 6 inches (50.8 to 152.4 mm) long and a third to half as wide. The width varies from tree to tree and sometimes on the same tree. Narrow leaves have rounded bases and slowly flare out to about the same width along the sides before rounding down to their tips. Broader leaves flare out to their widest a little past the midpoint and then round down to blunt tips. Both shapes have uniformly spaced, coarse teeth that point forward, have rounded tips, and often hook inward at the tips. The leathery leaf blade is a shiny yellow-green above and light green with minute hairs below. The side veins are straight and uniformly spaced, with each vein ending in a tooth. Acorns grow singly or in pairs on very short stalks. The mature acorn is medium to dark brown, ¾ inch (19.1 mm) long, and a little less than half covered by a thin cap.

Features: Chinkapin Oak is a small tree with little commercial value. It is reported to have the sweetest acorns of all the oaks, and they are eaten by a wide variety of wildlife.

Natural Range: Chinkapin Oak is generally found on limestone-derived soils and limestone outcrops. It grows on dry soils from New Hampshire west to Iowa and south to east Texas and the Florida Panhandle. It reaches its greatest size in the Ohio Valley.

Overcup Oak, *Quercus lyrata*
Swamp Post Oak, Swamp White Oak, Water White Oak

Overcup Oak is a medium-size southern tree that usually does not grow larger than 60 to 90 feet (18.3 to 27.4 m) in height and 2 to 2 ½ feet (.6 to .8 m) in diameter at breast height and is often much smaller. The bark is light brown to gray-brown in color, with long, narrow, uniformly shaped, flat-topped plates separated by narrow, slitlike, horizontal cracks. The trunk is often swollen at the base and crooked, twisting spirally up to the branches. The crown is filled with widely spaced, crooked branches that do not have many small secondary or fine branches.

Alternate leaves (page 83) are quite variable but usually are 6 to 8 inches (152.4 to 203.2 mm) long and 1 to 4 inches (25.4 to 101.6 mm) wide, with deep sinuses and five to nine rounded lobes. The base usually tapers gradually from a thin point to the widest lobes that occur about midway along the leaf. The two base lobes are usually much smaller than those farther out on the leaf. The leaf is thick and leathery, with a lustrous green surface on top and a pale green, sometimes fuzzy bottom surface. The acorns are distinctive, with scaly caps covering all but a small lower portion of the nuts.

Features: Overcup Oak lumber has little commercial value because of its spiral grain, frequent knots, and tendency to crack open during the drying process. When it does end up on the market, it is sold as low-quality white oak. It has found some use as an urban street tree. The acorns are eaten by a wide variety of wildlife. The common name is derived from the fact that the cap covers almost the entire acorn.

Natural Range: Overcup Oak is most often found growing in frequently flooded lowland areas, such as river bottoms or swamps. It grows in the wetter sites in the bottomlands of the coastal and Gulf plains from Delaware to East Texas. It also extends up the Mississippi River bottoms to southeastern Missouri, southern Illinois, southwestern Indiana, and western Kentucky.

Post Oak, *Quercus stellata*
Box White Oak, Iron Oak

Post Oak is a slow-growing, small to medium-size tree that seldom reaches more than 40 feet (12.2 m) tall and 1 to 2 feet (.3 to .6 m) in diameter at breast height. It can be recognized from a distance by its large, scattered, twisted limbs with dangling tips that make the tree look as if it were designed for a horror movie. The bark is laid out in tight, long, narrow, straight, horizontal, low ridges and shallow fissures. The pattern looks like thick hair that has just been combed out straight. As the tree ages, the bark darkens from light gray-white to a medium charcoal-gray, and the ridges begin to break into segments that are 2 to 6 inches (50.8 to 152.4 mm) long and rounded at both ends. Like several other members of the white oak group, Post Oak often has large, smooth, silver-gray patches of bark that make it look as if the surface bark has been scraped away. Unlike most of the other trees in this group, Post Oak bark does not peel away from the tree.

Leaves (page 83) are 1 ½ to 6 inches (38.1 to 152.4 mm) long and distinctive with their cross-shaped lobes. The two central lobes are larger than the others. The lower surface of rough textured leaf blade is usually hairy. Acorns are ⅜ to ¾ inch long (9.5 to 19.1 mm) and light brown.

Features: Post Oak is very drought-resistant, so it can grow on very dry, south- and west-facing, rocky soils. This ability to survive drought and grow in poor soils makes it a good choice for landscape planting on dry, challenging urban sites. The wood is marketed commercially as white oak. Acorns drop in the fall and are eaten by deer, turkeys, squirrels, and other rodents that are storing up fat for the winter.

Natural Range: Post Oak can be found growing naturally from the southern edges of the Great Lakes states through Massachusetts and southward to the shores of the Gulf of Mexico.

Southern Live Oak, *Quercus virginiana*
Virginia Live Oak, Spanish Oak

Southern Live Oak has widely spaced, spreading, crooked branches that are often massive and almost parallel to the ground, frequently spreading farther horizontally than the tree is tall, forming a tree that may reach 80 feet (24.4 m) tall and over 100 feet (30.5 m) wide at maturity. The tree can be quickly identified, regardless of age and size, by its long, twisting branches; strong trunk; dark, deeply furrowed bark; and evergreen leaves. The trunk is often short and sometimes forked. Diameter at breast height is 3 to 4 feet (.9 to 1.2 m) and is generally large for even oak species partly due to its buttressed trunk.

Leaves (page 51) are alternate, simple, 2 to 5 inches (50.8 to 127 mm) long by ½ to 2 inches (12.7 to 50.8 mm) wide, thick, leathery, and stiff, with pointed bases and rounded tips. The top leaf surface is dark green; the bottom is pale and usually thickly downy. Leaf edges often curl downward. Acorns are ⅝ to 1 inch (15.9 to 25.4 mm) long and dark brown to almost black.

Features: Ship and boat builders once prized Southern Live Oak trees for the keels and ribs of their boats, because it was very strong and, most important, precurved. Its fast early growth, ease of transplanting, and beautiful shape make it a favorite urban tree within its range. A wide variety of wildlife feeds on the acorns.

Natural Range: The natural range for Southern Live Oak is the sandy soils of the southern coastal plain from southeastern Virginia to southeastern Texas. This range has been expanded somewhat by urban plantings.

Swamp Chestnut Oak, *Quercus michauxii*
Cow Oak, Basket Oak

Swamp Chestnut Oak is a medium to large tree often reaching only 40 feet (12.2 m) in height and 1⅓ feet (.4 m) in diameter at breast height on upland sites, but it can grow over 100 feet (30.5 m) tall and 3½ feet (1 m) in diameter on well-drained alluvial floodplains. It develops a compact crown regardless of the site. In upland situations, the bark is very light gray. In lowlands, the bark is darker gray and often has a salmon pinkish cast when the sun hits it. Bark patterns vary. It can be tight with shallow, parallel valleys and narrow, flat-topped ridge plates; have no discernible valleys between plates that are flaking loose from any or all four sides; or have long, peeling side strips. In each case, the trunk bark pattern continues high into the crown before the limbs become smooth.

Leaves (page 78) are 4 to 8 inches (101.6 to 203.2 mm) long. The leathery blade is diamond-shaped, with the widest portion being approximately two-thirds of the way to the tip. Edges are coarsely wavy-toothed. The top surface is dark green and smooth, and the bottom is downy and pale. Acorns are 1 inch (25.4 mm) long and light brown.

Swamp Chestnut Oak, Chinkapin Oak, and White Oak can be very difficult to differentiate in winter, because their characteristics often overlap. It helps a little to remember that Swamp Chestnut Oak grows best in bottomlands that are periodically flooded, whereas Chinkapin and White Oaks do better on well-drained soils. Searching the ground for leaves is the best way to confirm that the tree is Swamp Chestnut Oak.

Features: The wood of Swamp Chestnut Oak is not separated out from the other white oaks in the lumber industry. It works well with tools, looks good, and can be used for almost anything made from wood, including baskets. Acorns are sweet.

Natural Range: Swamp Chestnut Oak can be found growing throughout the lower two-thirds of the eastern United States.

Swamp White Oak, *Quercus bicolor*
White Oak

Swamp White Oak is a large tree that grows to 100 feet (30.5 m) in height and may exceed 4 feet (1.2 m) in diameter at breast height. When it grows in the open, the crown becomes large and rounded, with many long, contorted, thick, branches. The bark is soft, moderately thick, and varying shades of gray. The bark pattern is long, narrow, flat-topped plates separated by narrow, vertical cracks. This pattern continues up into the crown and out along the major limbs.

Leaves (page 84) are 4 to 7 inches (101.6 to 177.8 mm) long and 2 to 4 ½ inches (50.8 to 114.3 mm) wide. The blade is narrow at the base and gradually flares to its widest point beyond the center, then tapers back down to a pointed tip. Leaf shapes vary. Some have several irregularly shaped, shallow lobes and sinuses; others have a single wavy, wide lobe on either side. When multiple lobes are present, they point noticeably forward. The upper surface of the leaf is dark glossy green; the lower surface is white with velvety hairs.

A quick way to positively identify Swamp White Oak is to look for acorns on the tree or acorn caps on the ground. The acorns are attached to the tree singly or in pairs by a stem called a peduncle that is 1 to 4 inches (25.4 to 101.6 mm) long. *Note:* The accompanying picture is of an immature acorn. Once the acorn matures, the cap covers a little over half to three-fourths of the nut, which is over 1 inch (25.4 mm) long.

Features: The Latin name for this tree refers to the two-colored leaf, which is green on top and white on the bottom. The wood is used commercially as white oak.

Natural Range: Swamp White Oak is usually found growing in periodically flooded lowlands. It is most abundant from Iowa and Missouri east to Pennsylvania. There are outlying populations in Kentucky, Tennessee, and North Carolina to the south and up the coast to Maine.

White Oak, *Quercus alba*
Eastern White Oak, Stave Oak, Forked-Leaf White Oak

White Oaks are often among the largest trees in the eastern forest. Given time, these long-lived trees have the potential to reach heights of 150 feet (45.7 m) and over 4 feet (1.2 m) in diameter at breast height. Those growing in forest situations often have tall, clean trunks and small to medium-size crowns. In the open, the tree usually develops a short trunk and a broad, rounded crown filled with massive, sometimes twisted limbs.

White Oak trees have some of the lightest-colored bark in the forest, typically very light gray. The texture varies from medium rough and tight, with no loose edges, to long strips cracking loose and peeling from the side. Sections of bark that are peeling loose from the side can be easily broken off. Sometimes the trunk bark will be tight while the bark on the limbs peels.

The leaves (page 85) are tough and vary in size and shape, but they always have rounded lobes and sinuses. The sinuses vary in depth from over halfway to the midvein to only one-fourth of the way. Both leaf surfaces and edges are smooth. Acorns are oblong and up to 1 inch (25.4 mm) long, with a shallow cap. The acorns mature and drop in the fall.

This tree and several others in the white oak group are all very similar, so it is helpful to remember that the White Oak species is most likely to be found growing in well-drained bottomlands or dry upland slopes. It can survive on all but the driest sites, but it will seldom be found growing in wet areas that frequently flood or have standing water.

Features: White Oak is one of the most commercially prized trees in the forest. It is used in manufacturing veneer and many other high-quality wood products. The pores of the wood are sealed, making it suitable to use in the manufacture of staves for wine and whiskey barrels. The acorns are eaten by many species of animals and birds.

Natural Range: White Oak is common throughout all of the eastern United States except the wetlands of Louisiana and the highest parts of New England.

OSAGE-ORANGE

Osage-Orange, *Maclura pomifera*
Bodark, Bois D'Arc, Hedge Apple, Horse Apple

Osage-Orange seldom reaches more than 40 feet (12.2 m) in height and 1½ feet (.5 m) in diameter at breast height. It is a small tree with character. The tree forks low to the ground and forms a rounded crown of heavy, twisted, tortured-looking, interlacing branches that arch up, over, and down toward the ground. Many of these branches have stout thorns at leaf junction points. The silver-gray to orange-brown bark is thick and fibrous, with long, narrow, forked ridges that are scaly on top separated by deep fissures filled with splintered bark fragments sticking out from the plate sides. Shaving or breaking off the surface bark will reveal a distinctive brick orange inner bark.

Leaves (page 53) are alternate, simple, and shaped like wide-bodied boats, with wedge-shaped bases, pointed tips, and smooth edges. They are 3 to 5 inches (76.2 to 127 mm) long and 2 to 3 inches (50.8 to 76.2 mm) wide, with slender leaf stalks, or petioles, that are 1 to 1½ inches (25.4 to 38.1 mm) long. Both the dark green upper surface and pale green lower surface are smooth. Fruit is a heavy, yellow-green ball with a pebbled surface, 3½ to 5 inches (88.9 to 127 mm) in diameter. It is filled with a large number of brown, nutlike seeds. If the fresh fruit is punctured, a milky white juice will ooze out and soon turn black.

Features: Osage-Orange has a rich history. Native Americans used the wood for archery bows. Early settlers planted rows of the trees as fences, and some believe it actually inspired the invention of barbed wire. Some people place the fruit in their basements as an effective insect repellent. When boiled in water, the deep orange wood releases a yellow tint that has been used to dye clothes. The distinctive wood is very rot-resistant, heavy, and durable. It is used for furniture, fence posts, and other small items in local markets.

Natural Range: Osage-Orange originally grew only in southeastern Oklahoma and east Texas, but it has been widely planted and escaped captivity throughout every state in the country.

PALMETTO

Sabal Palmetto, *Sabal palmetto*
Cabbage Palmetto, Carolina Palmetto

Sabal Palmetto grows to an average height of 40 feet (12.2 m) and 1⅙ feet (.4 m) in diameter at breast height. The silver-gray to brown trunk is limb-free and, unless trimmed, is covered with long, coarse, pointed, inter-woven, spikelike growths that curve up and outward, giving the trunk a very rough, bristly look. If a portion of the trunk has been pruned, it is brown and fibrous. The tree terminates at the top with a cluster of long palm leaves growing directly out of the main stem.

The evergreen, compound leaves (page 28) are huge, often 4 to 7 feet (1.2 to 2.1 m) long, and fan-shaped, with opposite rows of sword-shaped leaflets growing along a long central stalk that is flat on top and rounded on the bottom. The leaves all hang from clusters at the top of the tree and droop down the sides, giving Sabal Palmetto the classic palm tree look.

Features: Sabal Palmetto is a very popular ornamental plant within its range. Native Americans harvested the large terminal buds for food. Early colonists continued this practice for many years before they decided it was too destructive to a tree that was useful for many other things. During the Revolutionary War, Sabal Palmetto logs were used in Charleston, South Carolina, to fortify the walls of Fort Moultrie. When the British attacked the fort, their cannonballs bounced harmlessly off these tough logs, caus-ing the attack to fail. The wood has also been used for wharf pilings, docks, and poles, because sea worms do not attack it. Today the leaves are woven into baskets or brooms.

Natural Range: Sabal Palmetto is the only native palmetto that grows in the United States north of Florida. It can be found along a narrow coastal strip from southeastern North Carolina to Georgia and throughout Florida.

PAULOWNIA

Paulownia, *Paulownia tomentosa*
Empress Tree, Princess Tree, Royal Paulownia

Paulownia is an exotic, medium-size tree reaching 50 feet (15.2 m) in mature height and 2 feet (.6 m) in diameter at breast height. This non-native tree can be easily identified by its short trunk, clumsy umbrella-shaped top, large clusters of dangling seed capsules, and smooth, gray bark that has slightly raised patterns of wide, flat-topped, wavy lines reminiscent of the marks on a very large snake. Branches are widely scattered, smooth, and noticeably large for their length. They usually grow from the tree at right angles.

Paulownia leaves (page 53) are 5 to 12 inches (127 to 304.8 mm) long and wide. They are heart-shaped, usually with smooth, entire edges but sometimes slightly three-lobed. The leaf is slightly hairy on top and very hairy on the bottom. Clusters of upright flower buds bloom in spring, producing showy purple flowers. Tiny, hairy seeds develop on the inside linings of hollow wooden pods that grow in clusters and look like bunches of large, wooden grapes.

When the leaves are missing, Paulownia can be confused with another exotic tree called Ailanthus, which has similar bark and branches. But Ailanthus is usually tall, straight, and well-pruned, with short branches and no nutlike pods.

Features: Paulownia more than likely found its way into the United States during colonial times, when its fruit pods were used as packing materials for protecting fine dishes shipped from China. Despite its small size, Paulownia has a large commercial market for use in building many products, including fine furniture and musical instruments. It is also becoming popular with wood-carvers. When dried, the soft wood is very lightweight and remains stable even in high humidity.

Natural Range: Paulownia is native to China, but it has naturalized throughout most of the eastern United States.

PERSIMMON

Persimmon, *Diospyros virginiana*
Common Persimmon, Possum Wood

Persimmon is a small to medium-size tree usually reaching 20 to 75 feet (6.1 to 22.9 m) in mature height and 1 to 2 feet (.3 to .6 m) in diameter at breast height. It is a sun-loving tree that is often found growing out in the open or in fencerows where its rounded crown can take full advantage of the sun. The dark silver-gray to brown-black bark is noticeably thick and blocky. Young trees often have deep-fissured, sharp-edged, blocky bark. As the tree ages, the blocks stay about the same size, but the edges of the bark plates smooth over, making the bark look as though the edges of the individual plates were rounded off with sandpaper. The presence of fine, orange lines called lenticels scattered at random intervals on the small limbs and twigs can be used as a secondary means of identification.

Alternate, simple leaves (page 54) are 4 to 6 inches (101.6 to 152.4 mm) long. The leaf is oval with a rounded base and pointed tip, smooth edges, shiny dark green top, and paler green bottom. The petiole is ⅓ to 1 inch (8.5 to 25.4 mm) long and covered with tiny hairs. Fruit is a round, pulpy berry ¾ to 1 inch (19.1 to 25.4 mm) in diameter, with a hard seed at the core. It matures after frost, turning from green to purple-orange.

Features: Persimmon fruit will pucker the mouth when green, but after several hard frosts, it ripens into a very sweet purple-orange fruit that is enjoyed by a wide variety of animals. People have long harvested the fruit to make mouth-watering breads, jellies, puddings, and pies with the pulp. The very dense, hard wood has been traditionally used to make implements that have to take rough treatment, like golf-club heads or weavers' shuttles.

Natural Range: Persimmon can be found growing throughout the eastern United States.

PINE

Austrian Pine, *Pinus nigra*
European Black Pine

Austrian Pine is a medium-size evergreen that grows to about 60 feet (18.3 m) in height and 2 feet (.6 m) in diameter at breast height. Like the native Eastern White Pine and Red Pine, it grows a set of limbs each year in a whorled pattern around the trunk, resembling spokes reaching out at right angles from the hub of a wheel. There is a bare space on the trunk between each year's growth. The limbs form a large, thick, pyramidal crown filled with dark green, needlelike foliage. The ends of the branches turn slightly upward at the tips. The trunk bark is a dark gray to dull dark brown, with a rough but fairly thin surface of flat plates that get thicker with age.

The evergreen needles (page 21) are 3½ to 6 inches (88.9 to 152.4 mm) long and bundled in sets of two. They are slender, stiff, often shiny, and dark blue-green in color. Stalkless, egg-shaped cones are 2 to 3 inches (50.8 to 76.2 mm) long at maturity. After opening and shedding their seeds, the cones remain on the tree for several years before falling off.

In the northern states, the Austrian Pine is likely to be confused with the native Red Pine. The quickest way to distinguish between the two species is to look at the trunk bark color. Austrian Pine bark is dull brown, while Red Pine has a reddish brown color.

Features: The Austrian Pine tree was one of the first trees introduced into the United States, planted by homesteaders for protection from the sun, wind, and snow in the treeless Great Plains. It continues to be a favorite urban tree because of its tolerance to the salt and sulfur dioxide damage often encountered in large cities.

Natural Range: Austrian pine is native to Europe. First imported in the eighteenth century, it has been widely planted as an ornamental throughout the middle and eastern United States.

Eastern White Pine, *Pinus strobus*
White Pine, Northern White Pine

Eastern White Pine is the largest conifer in the eastern United States, often growing over 100 feet (30.5 m) in height and 3 to 4 feet (.9 to 1.2 m) in diameter at breast height. Like Austrian Pine and Red Pine, it grows a set of right-angled branches each year, resulting in a series of whorled branches clustered around the trunk at the same height on the tree, followed by a bare space, then another cluster. This wagon-wheel pattern repeats all the way to the top of the tree. When the tree is grown in plantations or forest situations, the lower limbs die off, often leaving whorls of dead branches or stubs sticking out of the trunk. Open-grown trees often hold their branches almost to the ground and look like large Christmas trees. Young bark is silver-gray and very smooth except for limb junctions, where the bark forms wrinkled rings around each limb. Older bark changes from a silver-gray to almost black and becomes quite rough, with well-defined plates and crevices.

Eastern White Pine is easy to identify by its deep blue-green needles (page 21) that grow five to a bundle and are 3 to 5 inches (76.2 to 127 mm) long. Its slender cones are 4 to 8 inches (101.6 to 203.2 mm) long, with flat, smooth scales. The cones often exude sap from the scales, making them very sticky. After maturing in midsummer to late summer, the cones dry out and open to release winged seeds.

Features: Eastern White Pine was at one time the most valuable conifer in the eastern United States. The wood is used for many construction purposes; its low shrinkage rate makes it especially valuable for building log cabins. Eastern White Pine is widely used for reforestation, featured urban trees, and Christmas trees.

Natural Range: The natural range for Eastern White Pine extends throughout the New England states westward to Minnesota and southward down the Appalachian Mountains to northern Alabama. It is now much more widespread because of extensive plantings throughout most of the eastern United States.

Jack Pine, *Pinus banksiana*
Bank Pine, Northern Scrub Pine, Gray Pine, Spruce Pine

Jack Pine is a scruffy-looking, little tree that usually grows 40 to 70 feet (12.2 to 21.3 m) in height and ⅔ to 1 foot (.2 to .3 m) in diameter at breast height. The trunk usually holds branches quite low to the ground. When the lower branches do die, they remain hanging from the trunk or break off and leave ragged stubs sticking out. The remaining branches spread out into a wide-based, slender-topped, ragged crown. The thin, scaly bark on the trunk is a dark gray to reddish brown, turning a brighter red toward the ends of the twigs.

Leaves (page 22) are evergreen needles that are 1½ to 2 inches (38.1 to 50.8 mm) long, dark green to grayish green, stiff, stout, slightly flat, and sometimes twisted. They are packaged in bundles of two needles that usually flare away from each other. The stalkless cones are one of the quickest means of identifying Jack Pine. The cone is 1 to 1½ inches (25.4 to 38.1 mm) long and usually has a tip that curves sharply toward the end of the twig. Most of the cones remain glued closed on the tree for many years, until the heat from a forest fire causes them to pop open and release their winged seeds.

Features: Jack Pine is harvested commercially for pulpwood lumber and round timber. Usually found growing in pure or mixed stands on dry areas that are too infertile for other trees to thrive, it is a pioneer species that comes in whenever mineral soils are exposed by a natural disturbance such as a forest fire.

Natural Range: Jack Pine is one of the northernmost pines, found growing along the Great Lakes and on the sandy coastal plain areas of New England. Its natural range in the United States is limited to Maine, New Hampshire, northern New York, northwest Indiana, northeast Illinois, Wisconsin, and Minnesota.

Loblolly Pine, *Pinus taeda*
Arkansas Pine, North Carolina Pine, Oldfield Pine

Loblolly Pine can reach large proportions, maturing at heights of 80 to 100 feet (24.4 to 30.5 m) and 2 to 4 feet (.6 to 1.3 m) in diameter at breast height. It is a southern evergreen with a gently sweeping, limb-free trunk and a top filled with upward-sweeping branches. The crown is made up of thick, soft, round tufts of pine needles at the ends of scattered branches, with daylight showing in between bunches of foliage. The bark is dark brownish gray, thick, chunky, and scaly. Bark plates are rough and rounded over on top. They are separated by deep, irregular fissures that often show a dark orange inner bark in the deepest cracks.

Needles (page 22) are 6 to 9 inches (152.4 to 228.6 mm) long, growing three to a bundle. They will bend double without breaking. Mature cones are 3 to 5 inches (76.2 to 127 mm) long, prickly barbed, and short-stalked. These cones remain on the tree in sets of one to three for quite some time after they open and shed their winged seeds. After they fall to the ground, they often take several months to deteriorate.

Features: Loblolly Pine is one of the most important southern yellow pines. It has been genetically improved for the fast, uniform growth needed for the commercial plantation production of pulpwood and sawlogs. Its fast growth and strong root system also make it a favorite pine for ornamental planting. Squirrels cut the green cones and eat the seeds.

Natural Range: The natural range of Loblolly Pine runs along the coastal plain from New Jersey to north Florida and east Texas. From North Carolina, it expands westward, looping under the Great Smoky Mountains and following along the southern edge of Tennessee before angling down into east Texas. Extensive planting has expanded the range northward through Tennessee into Kentucky.

Longleaf Pine, *Pinus palustris*
Georgia Pine, Hard Pine, Heart Pine, Southern Yellow Pine, Yellow Pine

Longleaf Pine often reaches more than 80 feet (24.4 m) in height and 2 ½ feet (.8 m) in diameter at breast height. It is a tall, straight conifer with an irregularly shaped, open crown of widely scattered limbs. The open canopy has about as much daylight present as there is foliage. The large buds growing on branch ends are covered with silver scales. On sunny days, these buds often reflect silver flashes in the canopy, making the tree sometimes seem to twinkle in the sunlight. The trunk is long, straight, and limb-free, with scaly bark plates that are large, flat, and irregularly shaped. The plates overlap one another without defined furrows. Peeling the surface will reveal clay brown to rust-red inner bark. The seedling goes through a "grass" stage, where it is simply a single short stalk topped with a moplike tuft of long needles.

Longleaf Pine needles (page 23) are noticeably long, measuring 10 to 16 inches (254 to 406.4 mm), and grow in bundles of three. At 6 to 10 inches (152.4 to 254 mm) long, the cones are overall the largest of any pinecones in the eastern United States. Winged seeds drop out of the cones in the fall.

Features: Longleaf Pine is a premier lumber tree that is grown and harvested for many different markets, including naval stores. The needles are raked, baled, and sold as pine straw mulch. For many years, the sap was collected and used in making turpentine and other chemical compounds. Today even the cones are harvested and sold to craftsmen.

Natural Range: Longleaf Pine can be found growing in the piedmont and coastal plain regions of southeast Virginia, North Carolina, South Carolina, Georgia, Florida, Alabama, Louisiana, and east Texas.

Pitch Pine, *Pinus rigida*
Bank Pine, Hard Pine, Jack Pine, Jersey Pine

Pitch Pine is a medium-size evergreen tree usually reaching 50 to 75 feet (15.2 to 22.9 m) in height and 1 to 2 feet (.3 to .6 m) in diameter at breast height. It has an irregularly shaped top and rough, brown, platy bark. Limbs generally grow horizontally and have twigs that are rough and bumpy.

The easiest way to identify Pitch Pine is its unique ability to grow bundles of needles directly out of its trunk. Short, stubby dwarf limbs are sometimes also present growing out of the lower trunk.

Needles (page 23) are evergreen, 3 to 5 inches (76.2 to 127mm) long, widespread, sharp-tipped, stout, stiff, and yellow-green. Stalkless, prickly cones are 1½ to 2 inches (38.1 to 50.8 mm), mature the second year, and often remain on the branches for several years after opening and shedding their seeds.

Features: The species name, *rigida,* means rigid or stiff and refers to both the needles and the cone scales. The wood of Pitch Pine is moderately strong and very resinous. It finds limited use as lumber. Because of this tree's ability to survive on very poor soils, it is often planted within its range to reforest barren areas where other trees cannot survive. Pitch Pine is one of very few pines with the ability to sprout a new stem from the trunk when the tree is broken off or cut down. The resin-soaked wood of stumps, called "rich wood," is prized for use as kindling to start fires because it lights easily and burns with intensity.

Natural Range: Pitch Pine principally occurs on poor, dry soils throughout the northern states, but it can also be found growing on the open ridgetops and south-facing slopes of the southern Appalachian Mountains. It grows from southern Maine to New York and extends down the Appalachians to north Georgia

Red Pine, *Pinus resinosa*
Norway Pine

Red Pine can grow to be over 125 feet (38.1 m) in height and 60 inches (1.5 m) in diameter at breast height, but it usually matures at 50 to 80 feet (15.2 to 24.4 m) tall and 2 to 3 feet (.6 to .9 m) in diameter. It has a tall, straight rounded trunk and a symmetrically oval crown. Like Eastern White Pine and Austrian Pine, the limbs grow in sets of clustered whorls that project from the trunk like the spokes of a wagon wheel and form a tight, rounded crown. One set of encircling branches is grown each year. As the years pass, new limb sets grow at the top of the tree, and the oldest and lowest die and fall off, making the lower part of the trunk a limb-free cylinder. The bark on young trees is orange and flaky. As the tree matures, the bark plates become long, broad, and flat-topped, with a reddish tinge. Shallow, ragged fissures separate the plates.

Needles (page 24) are 4 to 6 inches (101.6 to 152.4 mm) long and bound together in bundles of two. The dark yellow-green needles are slender, straight, and flexible, but they will readily snap in two when bent double. Cones are about 2 inches (50.8 mm) long.

Features: The wood is used for lumber, piling, poles, cabin logs, and a number of other products. The tree is widely planted throughout the Northeast for sand-dune and sand-blow control, windbreaks, snowbreaks, timber production, and Christmas trees. Stands of red pine are usually quite popular recreational areas.

Natural Range: Natural stands of Red Pine are confined to the northern parts of the United States. Its range extends from Maine westward to Minnesota and eastward to Wisconsin, Michigan, New Jersey, Connecticut, and Massachusetts. Isolated stands may also be found growing in northern Illinois and eastern West Virginia.

Shortleaf Pine, *Pinus echinata*
Shortleaf Yellow Pine, Southern Yellow Pine, Oldfield Pine, Shortstraw Pine, Arkansas Soft Pine

Shortleaf Pine can reach heights of 80 to 100 feet (24.4 to 30.5 m) tall and 1⅔ to 3 feet (.5 to .9 m) in diameter at breast height. It can be found growing in pure stands or as single trees mixed throughout the hardwood forest. The trunk is long, straight, and limb-free. Large, flat bark plates covering the trunk often have resin pockets present on the surface. Small but easily visible to the naked eye, they are usually round and indented in the center, with a slightly raised perimeter, having the appearance of tiny moon craters. The bark is yellowish brown to rusty brown, sometimes with a slight purplish cast.

The rounded treetop is made up of lateral to upward-facing branches holding thick, upturned clumps of needles that look as if they are standing on top of the branches or being held in the palms of upturned hands. Daylight is usually present between needle clumps. Twigs up to ½ inch (12.7 mm) thick break cleanly when bent.

Needles (page 25) are evergreen, blue-green, slender, flexible, 2¼ to 4½ inches (57.2 to 114.3 mm) long, and mostly in bundles of two, sometimes three. Winged seeds are borne in very short-stalked cones that are 1½ to 2½ inches (38.1 to 63.5 mm) long, conical when green, and egg-shaped after opening. Cones open and shed their seeds late in the summer and early in the fall. After opening, the cones remain attached to the tree for quite some time before dropping to the ground.

Features: Shortleaf Pine lumber is used for high-quality southern pine lumber as well as pulpwood. Squirrels cut the maturing cones and eat the seeds.

Natural Range: Shortleaf Pine has the widest range of all the southern yellow pines. It grows southward from southern Ohio and New York to Florida and west through Kentucky and Tennessee to eastern Oklahoma and Texas.

Slash Pine, *Pinus elliottii*
Cuban Pine, Pitch Pine, Swamp Pine, Southern Pine, Yellow Slash Pine

Slash Pine is a tall, straight southern tree that often reaches 60 to 100 feet (18.3 to 30.5 m) in height and 2 to 2 ½ feet (.6 to .8 m) in diameter at breast height. It has a long, limb-free trunk covered with large, flat, purple-brown to orange-brown bark plates and topped by a dense, rounded crown of dark green needles. Flaking off the outer bark surface reveals an inner bark that is often bright orange.

Needles (page 25) are dark green, lustrous, stiff, 6 to 10 inches (152.4 to 254 mm) long, and in bundles of two and three. They grow in clusters at the ends of otherwise bare orange-brown branches, often resembling brooms. Winged seeds are borne in cones that range from 5 to 8 inches (127 to 203.2 mm) long and grow tilted back toward the trunk. Many cones hang on the tree for more than a year before falling off.

Features: Because of its fast growth, desirable form, and natural resistance to southern pine beetles, Slash Pine is widely planted along the coastal plain for timber products. It has traditionally been grown and tapped for turpentine and other naval stores. The seeds are excellent food for many birds and small mammals. Its dense top provides cover for birds in inclement weather.

Natural Range: The natural range of Slash Pine is along the coastal plain from the southeastern corner of South Carolina throughout Florida and along the Gulf coastal plain to the Mississippi River in Louisiana. This range has been extended northward somewhat through plantings.

Table Mountain Pine, *Pinus pungens*
Hickory Pine, Mountain Pine, Prickly Pine

Table Mountain Pine is a scruffy-looking, small to medium-size tree that seldom grows larger than 50 feet (15.2 m) in height and 1⅙ feet (.4 m) in diameter at breast height. Its irregularly shaped crown is filled with twisted limbs and clusters of heavily barbed cones. The bark is reddish brown in color and furrowed into moderately thin, slightly rounded to flat-topped, scaly plates on the lower trunk, changing to thin, orange bark toward the top of the tree. Older trees develop wide, flat bark plates with distinctive scalloped edges. Neither Pitch Pine nor Virginia Pine, which grow in association with Table Mountain Pine, has this characteristic.

Needles (page 26) are evergreen, dark green, 1½ to 3 inches (38.1 to 76.2 mm) long, thick, and stiff, sometimes twisting and spreading out from one another. They grow in bundles of two. Cones are the single best way to identify this tree. They are short and fat, with thick, sharp-hooking barbs that look like miniature rhinoceros horns on the ends of the scales. A spiral pattern of horn-tipped scales is evident when looking down on the tip of the cone. Some cones require the heat from fire before they will open and their shed winged seeds.

Features: Table Mountain Pine is usually too rare and small to be commercially important, but it serves the critical function of reforesting high ridges that have been burned over. Stands of these trees can make fighting forest fires difficult, because the unopened cones heat up, catch on fire, and spring open, sometimes causing the fire to cross control lines. It is not unusual for burning cones to jump 3 feet (.9 m) off the ground and roll down the mountainside, spreading pine seed and fire as they go.

Natural Range: Table Mountain Pine is usually found growing above 2,500 feet (762.2 m) in elevation. The natural range of Table Mountain Pine is restricted to the southern mountains and the higher elevations of the piedmont from New York to Georgia.

Virginia Pine, *Pinus virginiana*
Field Pine, Jersey Pine, Spruce Pine

Virginia Pine is a short-lived, medium-size evergreen tree that usually grows to 60 feet (18.3 m) in height and 1 to 1½ feet (.3 to .5 m) in diameter at breast height. These trees usually grow up in a pure stand but sometimes mix with other pines or hardwoods. Distinguishing characteristics include thin, reddish brown, flaky bark and the evidence of many dead limb stubs up and down the trunk. The crown is fairly thin and of uniform density, instead of the heavy clumps of greenery with open spaces typically seen in most southern yellow pines. Looking up through the tree's canopy presents the overall effect of a consistently thin, soft, lacy, filtered light.

Needles (page 26) are 1½ to 3 inches (38.1 to 76.2 mm) long, dull green to yellowish green, slightly flattened, and often twisted. They grow in bundles of two, with the needles usually spreading out in a V shape from each other. Winged seeds are borne in cones that are 1½ to 2¾ inches (38.1 to 69.9 mm) long, narrowly egg-shaped when green, and rounded when opened. Cones grow in multiple clusters along the sides of the branches.

Features: The wood of Virginia Pine contains very long fibers, making it a premium source of pulpwood for paper. This tree is a pioneer species that colonizes disturbed sites and abandoned fields. It is short-lived and shallow-rooted. The life span of the typical stand is sixty to eighty years before it falls apart. When and if one or more large trees are lost in the center of the stand, the neighboring trees tend to topple over into the opening because of the loss of support. This domino effect continues until support is reestablished by leaning trees that are held up by those lying below them. In older stands of trees, it is common to find pockets of fallen trees that all point toward the center of the opening.

Natural Range: Virginia Pine grows in a wide belt from eastern New York and Pennsylvania southward through the uplands of northern Alabama and northeastern Georgia.

PONDCYPRESS

Pondcypress, *Taxodium ascendens*

Pondcypress has a potential life span that far exceeds five hundred years. It can grow over 100 feet (30.5 m) in height and 5 feet (1.5 m) in diameter at breast height, but it seldom reaches this size. Pondcypress is usually found growing in shallow ponds and swamps, with low-growing knees, knoblike projections sticking up out of the water, sometimes found surrounding the base. A young tree develops a soft conical shape. As the tree ages, the lower branches drop off, and the crown flattens out. The base of the trunk also swells and becomes deeply fluted, with rounded ridges and deep, narrow fissures. Bark is thin and reddish brown to tan on the young tree, becoming thick and fibrous and often peeling up from the bottom as the tree ages.

Pondcypress needles (page 16) are usually lime green, ¼ inch (6.4 mm) long, and loosely woven around thin, soft center twigs that gently curve out from the main branch like sea grass waving in ocean currents. Occasionally some of the needles on the tree may become two-ranked as on Baldcypress. In the fall, needles turn yellow then reddish brown and drop off. Round, rough-surfaced, gumball-size, silver-gray fruit balls develop over the summer. They open to release seeds in fall and drop off the tree soon after (see picture of Baldcypress on page 153).

Features: The wood from Pondcypress is not separated from Baldcypress for commercial purposes and is highly prized for many uses. Lumber from mature trees is rot- and termite-resistant, a feature not found in lumber from young trees. The unique root system allows this tree to stand firm in even the highest winds. Baldcypress is a larger, close relative that is much more common. These two trees look essentially the same during the winter. The best way to differentiate the two is through leaf identification in the summer.

Natural Range: Pondcypress naturally grows in water or moist areas, and its range wraps around the lowlands of the southern coastal states and extends up the Mississippi River valley to Tennessee and Kentucky.

POPLAR

White Poplar, *Populus alba*
Silver Leaf Poplar

White Poplar is a medium-size non-native tree that reaches 80 feet (24.4 m) in height and 2 feet (.6 m) in diameter at breast height. It can be quickly identified by its gently curving, light gray trunk with rough, dark gray bark at the bottom. It can be distinguished from other trees with smooth, light gray bark, such as the aspens and birches, by the thin-lined, triangular outlines around the limbs. Many trees also have multiple bark eruptions with a center vertical line dividing two half circles. These eruptions are often laid out in horizontal rows, three to four clusters long, and they may cover most of the light gray portion of the trunk. The trunk often grows in sweeping arches, with branches that are small and randomly placed.

Leaves (page 79) are alternate, simple, and coarsely toothed. They are 2 to 4 inches (50.8 to 101.6 mm) long and almost as wide. The upper surface is dark green, and the lower surface is covered with silvery white, woolly fuzz. Edges are wavy-toothed and often lobed like maple. The leaf stalk, or petiole, is also coated with a thick mat of silver-white hairs.

Features: White Poplar was a popular yard tree until septic systems became the norm and the tree's ability to clog drainage pipes became known. It is still periodically planted for its outstanding green-and-white leaves, but it more often will be found at old home sites or wherever it escaped and became established as a wild tree.

Natural Range: White Poplar was introduced into the United States from Europe and Asia. Today it may be found almost anywhere in the eastern United States as a result of extensive planting.

REDBUD

Redbud, *Cercis canadensis*
Judas Tree

Redbud is a small tree that usually reaches 20 to 25.4 feet (6.1 to 7.6 m) in mature height, with a crown that may be a little wider than the tree is tall. It is most often found growing in the understory of open woodlands. This tree usually forks low to the ground, with two or more major limb systems that spread into a wide, irregularly shaped crown. The crotch forms a very sharp V. Twigs are dark, thin, and shiny. The thin, scaly bark is dark gray with a purple cast. Thin, wide bark plates peel up from the sides and lower ends, giving the tree a scruffy look.

Leaves (page 55) are 2 to 6 inches (50.8 to 152.4 mm) long and almost as broad, forming a classic heart shape. Edges are smooth, and the tip is rather abrupt. The top of the blade is purple in the spring, slowly turning dark green throughout the summer and rusty red in the fall. The bottom of the leaf is a pale green. In the spring, the branches are covered with light pink flowers. Fruit is a thin, flat bean.

Features: Redbud is a popular urban tree, with many developed varieties. However, it is not a tree with a particularly long life—seldom living beyond 40 to 50 years. It is especially useful for planting under power lines, because it does not grow tall enough to get into the lines. In spring, the small but quite showy pink flowers give this otherwise drab tree its moment of brilliant beauty.

Natural Range: Redbud can be found growing naturally from Canada and New Jersey south to the Gulf of Mexico.

SASSAFRAS

Sassafras, *Sassafras albidum*
White Sassafras

Sassafras usually grows to be a medium-size tree that may reach only 30 to 60 feet (9.1 to 18.3 m) in height and 2 to 3 feet (.6 to .9 m) in diameter at breast height, although occasionally larger specimens can be observed. The largest-known Sassafras, in Owensboro, Kentucky, is more than three hundred years old and measures over 100 feet (30.5 m) tall and 6¾ feet (2.1 m) in circumference. The thick, rough, weathered, reddish brown to silver-gray colored bark often causes Sassafras to be confused with other trees, including Black Walnut. Slicing or breaking off the surface of the bark will reveal a pale orange inner bark. Smelling the fresh-cut slice will usually be rewarded with the distinctive Sassafras odor that resembles the smell of root beer. Young twigs are often forked, bright green, smooth, brittle, and aromatic, with patches of rough bark growing in random patches. Scraping the bark off the young twigs will release a pleasant spicy odor, and chewing it will provide a spicy taste. Limbs in the treetop are usually clustered and twisted into an unkempt-looking crown.

Leaves (page 86) are of 3 to 5 inches (76.2 to 127 mm) long and may be mixed, with leaves with no lobes, two lobes, and three lobes all growing together in the same crown. The edges are smooth, giving the lobed leaves the look of mittens.

Features: Sassafras has a long history of human use. Native Americans used the leaves for food flavoring, the sap for making medicines, and the durable wood for many everyday products. Pioneers followed in their path, boiling an extract from the roots that they mixed with molasses and fermented into a flavorful beer. Before medical restrictions forbade the commercial practice, sassafras roots were one of the principal ingredients in making modern, nonalcoholic root beer.

Natural Range: Sassafras grows throughout the eastern United States from the Great Lakes states to southern Florida. Isolated populations can also be found in New England.

SILVERBELL

Carolina Silverbell, *Halesia tetraptera*

Carolina Silverbell is a small tree that seldom reaches more than 35 feet (10.7 m) in height and 1 foot (.3 m) in diameter at breast height. It usually forks low to the ground and forms a broadly spreading top. The bark is multicolored. The tops of the plates are purple, and the cracks in the bark, which get deeper with age, are gray along their inner edges and have cinnamon brown bases. The small limbs and twigs are purple, with short, chalky white lines that turn brown as the cracks develop. Larger trees have rectangular squares on the lower trunk that are purple on top but flake off to expose tan inner bark.

Leaves (page 62) are 3 to 5 inches (76.2 to 127 mm) long and canoe-shaped, with a short leaf stalk, or petiole, and very finely toothed edges. The upper surface looks textured but is smooth to the touch. The lower surface is lighter and covered with fine, white hairs. The dangling, four-sided, slender-tailed, four-winged, papery-sacked fruit that develop during the summer resemble miniature Japanese lanterns. Because of their reportedly sour taste, fruit often can be found lying on the ground uneaten by wildlife during most of the winter.

Carolina Silverbell can usually be distinguished from its larger relative Mountain Silverbell by its smaller leaves and tendency to fork low to the ground.

Features: The silverbells gained their name from the beautiful white flowers that dangle like bells in early spring. Carolina Silverbell is planted as a feature tree in many urban situations.

Natural Range: Carolina Silverbell can be found growing from southern Illinois and West Virginia south to Florida.

Mountain Silverbell, *Halesia monticola*
Silverbell

Mountain Silverbell is usually a single-stemmed tree that may reach mature sizes greater than 80 feet (24.4 m) in height and 2 feet (.6 m) in diameter at breast height. The bark looks like the skin of a very old, petrified reptile. It is made up of very rough, rectangular, shiny, purple-hued smoke gray top plates that crack loose from all sides and peel off in stiff, paper-thin layers, exposing varying shades of tan inner bark. The pattern may be reminiscent of blocked milk chocolate bars. Branches are long and slender, forming an oval crown.

Leaves (page 62) are alternate, 8 to 11 inches (203.2 to 279.4 mm) long, spear-shaped, rounded at the base, pointed at the tip, and very finely toothed along the edges. The top looks textured but is smooth to the touch; the bottom is pale and slightly hairy. The dangling, four-sided, slender-tailed, four-winged, papery-sacked fruit that develop during the summer resemble miniature Japanese lanterns. Because of their reportedly sour taste, fruit can often be found lying on the ground uneaten by wildlife during most of the winter.

Mountain Silverbell can usually be distinguished from its smaller relative Carolina Silverbell by its much larger leaves, tree height, and the fact that it is usually single-stemmed.

Features: The silverbells gained their name from the beautiful white flowers that dangle like bells in early spring.

Natural Range: Mountain Silverbell can be found growing in the mountains of Tennessee, North Carolina, and Georgia. It reaches its greatest size in the Great Smoky Mountains National Park. The current park record is 112 feet (34.1 m) tall and 12⅔ inches (3.9 m) in circumference at breast height.

SMOKETREE

American Smoketree, *Cotinus obovatus*
Chittamwood

American Smoketree is a small tree that seldom grows taller than 35 feet (10.7 m) in height or larger than 12 inches (304.8 mm) in diameter at breast height. It is quite rare even within its range. The trunk is short, usually forking into a wide crown filled with long, widely spaced branches. The light gray to grayish brown bark on the trunk and larger branches is thin and flat, with flakes peeling up from the bottom edge. The bottom of the flakes is often rounded and overlapping, without discernible crevices. Twigs are marked with prominent whitish corky lenticels and have continuous pith centers. When crushed, the twigs release a distinctive odor and gummy sap.

Alternate, egg-shaped leaves (page 45) are 2 to 6 inches (50.8 to 152.4 mm) long and 1 ½ to 3 inches (38.1 to 76.2 mm) wide, with a dull green upper surface and lighter lower surface that is covered with hairs when young, becoming smooth later in the summer. Crushed leaves give off a distinctive mint odor. The long, hairy fluffs of pink flowers look from a distance like puffs of smoke, giving the tree its name.

Features: American Smoketree finds limited use as an ornamental planting, where it is valued for its distinctive smoky-plumed flowers and dark red fall color. During the Civil War, Southern uniforms were colored with a yellow-brown dye extracted from the dark yellow wood of this tree.

Natural Range: This rare tree grows on rock bluffs and in limestone glades from east Tennessee and northern Alabama westward to Arkansas, Missouri, Oklahoma, and Texas.

SOURWOOD

Sourwood, *Oxydendrum arboreum*
Sorrel-Tree

Sourwood is a small tree that is usually less than 50 feet (15.2 m) in height and 1 foot (.3 m) in diameter at breast height. It often grows with an arching trunk and a top that droops over. The silver-gray to reddish brown bark is very thick and chunky. The bark is deeply furrowed with the appearance of narrow and scaly ridges. On older and larger trees, these bark ridges are often divided horizontally, giving the bark a blocky appearance. One-year-old twigs often take the form of long, slender, bright red whips.

Leaves (page 63) are alternate, lance-shaped, 4 to 7 inches (101.6 to 177.8 mm) long, and 1 to 2 inches (25.4 to 50.8 mm) wide, with finely toothed margins. Fine hairs stick up along the bottom of the center vein when the leaf is folded back in half along this vein. The leaf has a deep green, smooth upper surface and a lighter surface below. Leaves have a very sour taste when bitten or chewed. In spring, Sourwood produces upright clusters of showy flowers at the ends of the limbs. These clusters later develop small, five-sided fruit capsules whose weight causes the clusters to arch over and hang down. The fine-textured clusters of dried fruit and fruit stems hang from the tree throughout most of the winter.

Features: Sourwood makes a beautiful feature tree in urban settings. It is attractive in all seasons, with clusters of white flowers in the spring, followed by gracefully drooping foliage that turns a deep red in the fall, as well as its deeply furrowed bark. Bees collect pollen from the showy spring flowers to make sourwood honey.

Natural Range: Sourwood ranges from Louisiana and Mississippi north and east to southern Indiana and Pennsylvania.

SPRUCE

Blue Spruce, *Picea pungens*
Colorado Blue Spruce, Colorado Spruce, Silver Spruce

Blue Spruce is an evergreen that is native to the western United States. It is included in this book because of its popularity as a featured planted tree in urban settings throughout the eastern part of the country. In the West, Blue Spruce can grow over 100 feet (30.5 m) tall, but in eastern urban settings, it grows slowly, reaching an average of 30 to 50 feet (9.1 to 15.2 m) in height in fifty years.

The tree is pyramidal in form, but as it gets older, it becomes more open, droopy, and irregular in shape. In urban plantings, the tree typically holds its branches all the way to the ground. The dark gray trunk bark is thin and flaky, with overlapping flat flakes. The branches are bright orange-brown and covered on all sides with stiff, blue-green to silver-green needles. The needles (page 18) are ¾ to 1¼ inches (19.1 to 31.8 mm) long, four-sided, and sharply incurved. They release a sharply acid flavor if chewed. Winged seeds are borne in cones that are cylindrical but tapered slightly at each end. The cones are 2 to 4 inches (50.8 to 101.6 mm) long and shiny brown, with irregular scales.

Features: Blue Spruce is valued mainly for its ornamental value as a featured yard tree. It is also sold as a Christmas tree.

Natural Range: Blue Spruce is native to the central and western Rocky Mountains of the western United States, but it is now extensively planted throughout the eastern United States as an ornamental.

Norway Spruce, *Picea abies*

Norway Spruce is a small to medium-size evergreen averaging less than 80 feet (24.4 m) in height and 1⅔ feet (.5 m) in diameter at breast height. Its drooping branches and large, downward-hanging cones can quickly identify Norway Spruce. Major branches curve upward like outstretched arms and uplifted hands, with secondary branches hanging down like the long leather fringe of a great Native American warrior's ceremonial shirt. Branches are smooth and brown. Trunk bark is reddish brown to ash gray, thin, and cracked into variable scaly plates that sometimes peel in thin curls.

The evergreen needles (page 19) are ½ to 1 inch (12.7 to 25.4 mm) long, four-sided, dull green, lustrous, and sharp-pointed. They grow from the stem on very short, peglike bases. Winged seeds are borne in cones that are 4 to 6 inches (101.6 to 152.4 mm) long. After releasing their cargo of winged seeds, the cones usually continue to hang on the tree for quite some time.

Features: Norway Spruce, with its characteristic drooping branches, has been used extensively as an evergreen windbreak and as a Christmas tree. It is also widely planted as an ornamental tree, particularly as a specimen yard tree.

Natural Range: Norway Spruce is native to Europe but has been planted throughout the eastern United States since colonial times.

Red Spruce, *Picea rubens*

Red Spruce is a small to medium-size tree that may reach 50 to 80 feet (15.2 to 24.4 m) in height and 1 to 2 feet (.3 to .6 m) in diameter at breast height.

Branches are generally close to one another along the main trunk, grow straight out from the trunk, and have a gently upward-sweeping form. The bark on the trunk is thin and gray, often with lichens growing over most of the surface.

Red Spruce can be identified by its needles (page 19), which are shiny yellow-green on all sides and point out in every direction like porcupine quills. They are ⅜ to ⅝ inch (9.5 to 15.9 mm) long, stiff, sharp-pointed, awl-shaped, and four-sided. These four-sided needles will not roll between the fingers. Pulling needles from the twig will result in bark tearing away with the needle, leaving a short post on the branch.

The small, winged seeds are borne in cones that are about 1¾ inches (44.5 mm) long. These cones are reddish brown in color, have smooth-edged scales, and hang down on small pegs. Few if any old cones will be found hanging on the tree, because they generally fall within the first year. This absence of old cones is a good way to distinguish Red Spruce from Black Spruce, which it closely resembles and often crosses to form hybrids. Also, if a spruce is found growing in a natural setting south of New York State, the tree is probably Red Spruce, because it alone ranges southward through the mountains of North Carolina and Tennessee.

Features: Red Spruce may live to be more than four hundred years old. Its wood is lightweight, straight-grained, and resilient. These attributes make it an important lumber tree that is used for many commercial purposes. Because of its natural resonance, it is often used for the sounding boards of musical instruments. Unlike Blue Spruce, the wood has no flavor.

Natural Range: Red Spruce grows from Canada southward through the mountains of North Carolina, Tennessee, and Georgia.

White Spruce, *Picea glauca*
Canadian Spruce, Skunk Spruce, Cat Spruce

White Spruce is a medium to large tree that can grow to a height of 100 feet (30.5 m) tall and 2 feet (.6 m) in diameter at breast height. The light brown bark is thin and has a whitish inner bark. It often oozes sticky sap that runs down its surface. Crushing its needlelike foliage releases a pungent odor, usually providing quick identification.

The blue-green evergreen needles (page 20), with white lines along the bottom, are ½ to ¾ inch (12.7 to 19.1 mm) long, and four-sided. They look as if they are all growing on top of the branch because the lower needles turn sharply upward and wrap around the twig, blending with those growing on the top surface. Winged seeds are borne in light brown cones that are 1 ½ to 2 ½ inches (38.1 to 63.5 mm) long and attached directly to the bottom of the branches.

Features: White Spruce is a commercially important northern tree. Its lightweight, straight-grained, resilient wood is harvested for lumber and pulpwood products.

Natural Range: White Spruce is primarily a Canadian tree whose range crosses over into the eastern United States in Minnesota and Maine.

SWEETGUM

Sweetgum, *Liquidambar styraciflua*
Bilsted, Redgum, Sapgum, Star-Leaf Gum

Sweetgum is a large tree with the potential to grow over 80 feet (24.4 m) in height and 4 feet (1.2 m) in diameter at breast height. Open-grown trees have a pyramidal crown filled with long, narrow branches growing out at right angles to the trunk. Trees grown in forest situations have long, limb-free trunks and small tops. The trunk has light gray, thick, rough, corklike bark, with long, narrow, rounded, flaky ridges and deep, narrow valleys. Many of the smaller twigs may have one or two opposite corky ridges growing along their length. Both the twigs and leaves release a distinct, pleasant odor when crushed, scraped, or broken. Buds are resin coated and glossy.

Leaves (page 93) are alternate, simple, 4 to 7 inches (101.6 to 177.8 mm) long, and almost that wide. Their lobes have a distinctive five-pointed star shape, with deep V-shaped sinuses and long, pointed lobes. The edges are finely toothed. The shiny, dark green blade has five major veins radiating out from the leaf stalking, or petiole. Fall leaf color varies from yellow to a deep purplish red. The fruit capsules are usually about the size of a golf ball and look like starbursts on a stem because of their sharp, open points sticking out in all directions. Some of these fruit capsules can usually be found hanging in the top of the tree throughout the winter.

Features: Sweetgum is commercially important as a lumber tree. The wood is used in the manufacture of many products, including fruit crates, and it is often the core stock in upholstered furniture. Many varieties of this tree have been developed for planting in urban situations.

Natural Range: With the exception of mountainous areas, Sweetgum can be found growing throughout the eastern United States from the Gulf of Mexico to Kentucky and Virginia. It is a lowland tree that prefers growing in moist to damp but well-drained bottomland soils.

SYCAMORE

Sycamore, *Platanus occidentalis*
Buttonwood, Buttonball-Tree, American Plane Tree

Sycamore is among the largest trees in the eastern United States, with the potential to reach 175 feet (53.4 m) in height and 8 feet (2.4 m) in diameter at breast height. Sycamore trees often fork low and spread out, with huge, open crowns. Both the trunk and the well-spaced, large, long limbs shed random patches of paper-thin, light tan bark, exposing large areas of smooth greenish gray to silver-white bark. The trunks of very large trees may eventually be covered with this light tan outer bark, but the limbs will continue to shed. The twigs are slender and form a zigzag pattern, with a bud on the outside edge of each turning point.

Leaves (page 94) are 4 to 8 inches (101.6 to 203.2 mm) long and almost as wide, alternate, simple, and fan-shaped, with three to five broad, toothed lobes with pointed tips. The upper surface is smooth. The lower surface begins the summer with a heavy coating of woolly, white hair, but as the season progresses, this hairy mat sloughs off, leaving the lower surface smooth by fall. The leaf stalk, or petiole, is usually hairy and has a hollow base that completely covers the twig bud.

The fruit is a brown ball of closely packed, needlelike seeds. It is long-stemmed and 1 inch (25.4 mm) in diameter. When the seeds mature, the ball slowly disintegrates, releasing a few seeds at a time until nothing is left but the stem to which they were attached. Sycamore balls are often present all winter long.

Features: The interlocking grain of Sycamore makes its wood difficult to work with tools and limits its commercial use for most wood products, but it finds its place as the wood from which butcher blocks are made. It is occasionally planted as an urban tree but is more likely to be planted along waterways to control erosion.

Natural Range: The native range for Sycamore covers every state in the eastern United States except Minnesota.

TUPELO

Black Tupelo, *Nyssa sylvatica*
Blackgum, Pepperidge, Sourgum, Tupelo, Tupelogum

Black Tupelo is a medium to large tree that may mature anywhere from 50 to 100 feet (15.2 to 30.5 m) in height and 2 to 3 feet (.6 to .9 m) in diameter at breast height. The silver-gray to almost black bark of the larger trees often so closely resembles the bark of oak or elm that at first glance the tree may be misidentified. Looking up, however, will reveal a crown filled with unusually small and slender, relatively short, often twisted branches growing out of the tree trunk at 90-degree angles. It often looks like an oak tree that had a bad hair day. The lower branches of younger trees often droop dramatically, especially if the tree is exposed to enough sunlight to encourage side growth. The bark is thick and narrowly fissured, with crevices breaking up the plates into long, narrow, vertical, interlocking sections. The bark on older trees flattens along the top of the plates.

Alternate leaves (page 55) are 2 to 5 inches (50.8 to 127 mm) long, oval, spear-tip–shaped, smoothed-edged, and shiny dark green. A short, narrow tip that often curls to the side or down projects from the broadly round leaf end. The leaves are evenly spaced along the entire new year's twig growth, with each leaf stalk, or petiole, turning upward from the stem before arching over and holding the arched leaf about 1 inch (25.4 mm) above the twig. Because of this, looking at the leaves from the end of the branch can sometimes give the illusion of a large daddy longlegs spider that is walking away. Fruit is a small, blue berry hanging from a short stem.

Features: Black Tupelo makes a very good-looking tree in an urban setting. This is especially true in fall, when the leaves turn a deep, crimson red. Many birds and small mammals eat its berry fruit. Bees make a uniquely flavorful honey from the flowers.

Natural Range: Black Tupelo is widespread throughout the eastern United States.

Swamp Tupelo, *sylvatica* var. *biflora*
Swamp Blackgum

Swamp Tupelo is often found growing as a small tree, but it has the potential to reach over 80 feet (24.4 m) in height and 3 feet (.9 m) in diameter at breast height. Larger trees develop a pronounced swelling at the base. The bark is silver-gray to almost black, with roughly rectangular, chunky plates separated by narrow, crooked furrows. The top of the tree is filled with small branches that often grow at almost right angles, forming an open, tall, but unkempt, thin crown.

Leaves (page 56) are alternate and thick-textured, with short leaf stalks, or petioles. The blade is 1½ to 4 inches (38.1 to 101.6 mm) long and ½ to 1½ inches (12.7 to 38.1 mm) wide. The smooth edges flare from a narrow base to the widest measurement past the midpoint, and then round down to a short-tipped end. The upper surface is a lustrous green, and the lower surface is paler and more or less covered with hairs. Fruit is purple-black, sour-tasting, and ¼ to ½ inch (6.4 to 12.7 mm) long, with a hard seed that has distinct ridges.

Swamp Tupelo is often found in southern swamps along with its close kin Water Tupelo. When leaves are present, it can be distinguished from Water Tupelo by its much smaller leaves.

Features: Bees visit Swamp Tupelo and harvest the flower pollen to make highly prized tupelo honey. Even though the fruits are sour, they are eaten by a wide variety of wildlife. The wood is not commercially important but is sometimes used locally for products that require a soft wood that is resistant to splitting.

Natural Range: Swamp Tupelo seems to prefer to grow standing in shallow, moving water and thus is often found in swampy areas. It can be found growing in the coastal swamps from Maryland to Florida and westward to east Texas. It also grows up the Mississippi River bottoms north to Southern Illinois.

Water Tupelo, *Nyssa aquatica*
Tupelo Gum, Cotton Gum, Water Gum

Water Tupelo is a large tree that can reach more than 100 feet (30.5 m) in height and 4 feet (1.2 m) in diameter at breast height. It is found growing in periodically flooded swamplands. In summer, these trees may stand on dry ground, but in the fall and winter, they are often covered by more than 3 feet (.9 m) of water for months at a time. The base of the tree is usually swollen, with a trunk that tapers to a long, narrow crown of small, short, scattered, drooping limbs. The bark is silver-gray to almost black, with narrow crevices separating chunky, round-topped, roughly rectangular plates. The edges of the bark plates are usually rounded over.

The alternate leaves (page 56) are 4 to 6 inches (101.6 to 152.4 mm) long and 2 to 4 inches (50.8 to 101.6 mm) wide. The outline is that of a wide-bodied boat, beginning with a rounded base that flares to parallel sides and rounds down to a short tip. Occasionally, widely spaced, coarse teeth break this shape. The leaf blade is thin, with a smooth, glossy upper surface and a paler, more or less fuzzy lower surface. The edges are smooth. Fruit is 1 inch (25.4 mm) long and purple-black, containing a large, smooth seed.

Features: Water Tupelo flowers are a favorite of bees for making honey. The dependable heavy crop of seeds each year is eaten by a wide variety of wildlife. This tree is harvested and used in manufacturing a wide variety of products requiring light and spongy wood that is resistant to splitting. Before plastics, it was used for making such specialty items as bottle corks and fishing-net floats.

Natural Range: Water Tupelo grows naturally in the swamps and coastal lowlands from North Carolina to Florida and along the Gulf to east Texas. It also extends up the Mississippi River bottoms to Illinois.

WALNUT

Black Walnut, *Juglans nigra*
Eastern Black Walnut, American Walnut

Black Walnut is a medium to large tree, maturing 70 to 90 feet (21.3 to 27.4 m) tall and 2 to 4 feet (.6 to 1.2 m) in diameter at breast height. It has a very rough, dark chocolate brown, sometimes silver-tinged bark and an open crown consisting of a few widely spaced, strong-looking limbs. Removing the relatively soft surface bark on the trunk of the tree will expose smooth, chocolate brown inner bark and release a distinctive odor. Splitting open a twig will reveal a chambered pith.

When present, the aromatic leaves (page 103) are 12 to 24 inches (304.8 to 609.6 mm) long and compound, with thirteen to twenty-three sharply toothed and pointed leaflets that are smooth on both surfaces. The terminal leaflet may be missing. Large nuts are covered with green, textured husks that turn black after the maturing nuts fall to the ground. The juicy husks readily stain anything they touch a dark brown color, and the stain is difficult to remove.

Features: The reddish brown to dark chocolate brown heartwood of Black Walnut is quite durable, even when in contact with the soil, and has been highly prized by cabinetmakers for centuries. The tree's nuts are among one of the few fruits of which all are used. The oily nuts are edible and have a strong flavor. Chemicals in the soft husks surrounding the shells are extracted for commercial use, and the nut hulls are crushed for use in manufacturing abrasives. This strong demand has resulted in Black Walnut becoming one of the trees most often planted in hardwood plantations.

Natural Range: Black Walnut grows as scattered individual trees from Illinois and Indiana east to New York and south through the piedmont sections of South Carolina, Georgia, Alabama, Arkansas, and Louisiana. With the exception of the Mississippi River bottoms, Black Walnut grows westward into Texas, Oklahoma, and the eastern edge of the Great Plains.

WHITE-CEDAR

Atlantic White-cedar, *Chamaecyparis thyoides*
Southern White-cedar, Coast White-cedar

Atlantic White-cedar is a medium-size tree that often reaches 50 to 70 feet (15.2 to 21.3 m) in height and ⅚ to 1⅔ feet (.3 to .5 m) in diameter at breast height. The trunk is usually straight and tall, but the tree occasionally may have a side limb that curves up, forming a wide fork and becoming a second trunk. The trunk bark is thin and stringy, with a silver-gray to reddish brown surface and a brick red inner color. The bark on larger trees develops long, flat, stringy plates that are separated by shallow furrows. The tree's evergreen crown is usually shaped like a tall spire, with slightly upturned, short branches holding thick clumps of foliage. Daylight can often be seen in the crown between the foliage clumps.

The slightly prickly leaves (page 13) are tiny, blue-green scales wrapped around sets of slender twigs. Each subset of scale-covered twigs grows on a flat plane, but instead of the sets lying on top of one another in layers, they twist, turn, and face in all directions. Often the subsets are positioned at right angles to one another.

The fruit is ½ to ¾ inch (12.7 to 19.1 mm) in diameter, a fleshy, globular, silver-gray colored cone with spiked protrusions on its surface. The plates of the mature fruit separate from one another, opening horizontal cracks that release the seed before drying out, turning dark brown, and falling from the tree. The opened cone resembles a set of shields that face away from one another and are tied together in the center.

Features: The Atlantic White-cedar is harvested commercially for its rot-resistant, lightweight wood. It is used for many purposes, including boat-building and wooden pipes for pipe organs. It is also highly prized as an ornamental tree.

Natural Range: Atlantic White-cedar grows along a narrow stretch of Atlantic and Gulf coastal plain from New England to Louisiana, most often found in freshwater swamps and bogs.

Northern White-cedar, *Thuja occidentalis*
Eastern White-cedar, Swamp-cedar

Northern White-cedar is a medium to large evergreen tree. Although it has the potential to grow much larger, it usually reaches only 40 to 50 feet (12.2 to 15.2 m) tall at maturity and 1 to 2 feet (.3 to .6 m) in diameter at breast height. The tree trunk is long and tapered, supporting a long, narrow, spirelike evergreen top that grows along the upper two-thirds of the trunk. If the top is damaged, the tree may respond by developing a second trunk that forks out and then upward. The silver-gray to charcoal-gray bark is thin and shredded, divided by shallow cracks into long, narrow plates. Peeling the surface bark will reveal a light chestnut brown inner bark. The relatively short, slender side branches grow from the main trunk at wide angles. The lower branches may droop slightly with age.

The evergreen leaves (page 14) are dark green and very smooth. They are scalelike and grow on four sides of the center twig, forming a pattern similar to that of a herringbone gold bracelet or necklace. The scale-covered twigs form flat, fan-shaped sprays of foliage, beginning with a single stem and then spreading out like flat fans stacked on top of one another in flat layers. Fruit is borne in erect cones that are ½ inch (12.7 mm) long and look like wooden flowers when the bracts are open and the seeds dispersed.

Features: The wood of Northern White-cedar is lightweight, aromatic, and rot-resistant. It is traditionally used to build small boats and other items that are exposed to the weather. Native Americans used the foliage to treat scurvy. Today the extracted oil from the crushed foliage is used in various medicines. Deer browse on the twigs and use the shelter provided by these trees for deeryards during severe winters.

Native Range: Northern White-cedar grows throughout much of Canada, extending southward along the Great Lakes and New England. There are also local populations of Northern White-cedar growing along the Appalachian and Cumberland Mountains.

WILLOW

Black Willow, *Salix nigra*
Swamp Willow, Gooding Willow, Willow

Black Willow is a moderately large tree that reaches 60 to 100 feet (18.3 to 30.5 m) in mature height and 1½ to 3 feet (.5 to .9 m) in diameter at breast height. It is very intolerant of shade and will most often be found growing alone or in pure stands in full sunlight, either in wet bottomland areas or beside bodies of water. It often has a short trunk or is forked low to ground, with multiple leaning, crooked trunks and irregularly shaped crowns. Trunk bark thickens with age, changing from thin and reddish brown to thick, brownish black, long, interlaced, scaly-topped ridges divided by deep, narrow, wandering furrows. The bark on old trees develops a shaggy look. In winter, the long, shiny, bright reddish brown to burnt orange twigs usually stand out. Twigs break off easily only at the base.

Leaves (page 63) are alternate, simple, and are bright green on both top and bottom surfaces. They are 4 to 6 inches (101.6 to 152.4 mm) long and less than ½ inch (12.7 mm) wide. Edges are finely toothed from base to tip, with tiny, yellow glands at or just under the tip of each tooth.

Features: Black Willow is a common tree that usually grows near water. Possibly its greatest contribution is its ability to control bank erosion by sprouting new trees from broken branches that lodge downstream. Black Willow produces salicin, the active ingredient in aspirin, and Native Americans reportedly chewed the tree's twigs to treat headaches.

Natural Range: Black Willow can be found growing throughout the eastern United States.

Weeping Willow, *Salix babylonica*

Weeping Willow is a graceful non-native tree that may reach 30 to 40 feet (9.1 to 12.2 m) in mature height and 7 feet (2.1 m) in diameter at breast height. The crown forms an oval top, with vertical sides drooping almost to the ground. This tree's quickest all-season identifying feature is its long, slender, yellowish brown, gracefully dangling twigs that may be over 6 feet (1.8 m) long and hang from the tree like a full head of long hair. The trunk is usually short, soon forking into two or more major branches. The bark is dark brown and very rough-textured, with long, vertical plates divided by ragged crevices.

The alternate leaves (page 65) are 2 ½ to 5 inches (63.5 to 127 mm) long and only ¼ to ½ inch (6.4 to 12.7 mm) wide, with very fine, sharp teeth along the edges. They are dark green above and whitish or gray below.

Features: Today's Weeping Willow is the result of years of being grown as a popular feature tree. It has lost some of the characteristics of the original parents that were introduced into the United States in the late 1700s. Many varieties have been developed since that time, leading to today's common form.

Natural Range: Weeping Willow is an exotic originally introduced from China that has been widely planted throughout the eastern United States. It is most common in the southeastern states and is often found next to water sources.

White Willow, *Salix alba*
European White Willow

White Willow is a medium-size tree that reaches 50 to 80 feet (15.2 to 24.4 m) in mature height and 2 to 3 feet (.6 to .9 m) in diameter at breast height. The tree may have one or more short, curved trunks that are covered with rough, gray-brown bark. The bark texture is reminiscent of whipped icing on a tall cake. Twigs are golden yellow to olive brown, smooth, and very flexible. They are often silky in spring and early summer.

The deciduous leaves (page 65) are 2 to 4 ½ inches (50.8 to 114.3 mm) long and ⅜ to 1¼ inches (9.5 to 31.8 mm) wide. They are slender with fine, sharp teeth along the edges. The blade is glossy green on top and silver-white below. Fine, silky hairs cover the lower surface and in some cases the upper surface as well.

Features: White Willow was originally planted for urban purposes and as windbreaks. The flexible branches are sometimes used to weave baskets. It is most likely to be found around cities.

Natural Range: White Willow is native to Europe and was introduced into the United States during colonial times. Several varieties have been developed and planted throughout the eastern United States, where it escaped cultivation and is now naturalized along many streams and in wet areas.

YELLOW-POPLAR

Yellow-Poplar, *Liriodendron tulipifera*
Tulip Poplar, Tuliptree, White-Poplar, Whitewood

Yellow-Poplar can grow very large, exceeding 120 feet (36.6 m) in height and 6 feet (1.8 m) in diameter. It is a distinctive tree that usually grows gun-barrel straight and round. On small trees, the bark is smooth and mouse gray, with shallow, white furrows. It becomes rougher and more silver-gray to butternut brown as the tree grows larger. On all but the largest trees, the bark usually looks as if it were molded on the tree, rather than cracking away as the tree grew.

Identification is relatively easy with the presence of what looks like white to silver-white chalk dust inside the channels and depressions of the bark. This dusting occurs on the trunk from the ground to the treetop. Younger trees instead have silver-lined cracks in the gray bark. Branches generally look small in relation to trunk size.

Alternate leaves (page 93) are 3 to 8 inches (76.2 to 203.2 mm) long and have four pointed lobes forming a distinct tulip shape. Yellow-Poplar leaves are 3 to 8 inches (76.2 to 203.2 mm) wide. They are as broad as long. The central leaf vein ends at the midpoint of the center sinus. Buds are flat and shaped like a duck's bill or drum major's hat. In the spring, large, beautiful, orange and pink, tulip-shaped flowers bloom. The pollinated flowers then develop seed cones that are 2 to 3 inches (50.8 to 76.2 mm) long, tapered, and erect. The cones fall apart over the winter as the seeds, which are 1 inch (25.4 mm) long and winged, drop from the stalk. Eventually only the upward-pointing, tapered cores are left standing on twig tips.

Features: Yellow-Poplar is an important timber tree that is used in manufacturing many different products. Its fast growth, strong root system, and beautiful form and flowers make it a popular shade tree for large areas. Bees use the flower pollen in making honey. Small animals feed on the seeds, and deer browse on the twigs and small seedlings.

Natural Range: Yellow-Poplar grows throughout the eastern United States from southern Michigan and New England south to the Gulf of Mexico.

YELLOWWOOD

Yellowwood, *Cladrastis kentukea*

Yellowwood is a small to medium-size tree that seldom grows larger than 50 feet (15.2 m) in height and 1⅔ feet (.5 m) in diameter at breast height. It typically forks low to the ground and forms a wide-spreading top that is often wider than the tree is tall. The bark is usually light gray in color, but in some moist situations, it may become almost black. It is very smooth, thin, and hard, often with horizontal wrinkles circling under branches and spots where branches once grew. These patches of wrinkles sometimes give the illusion that the bark is sagging slightly. Smooth branches are long, slender, and zigzag-shaped, with either a leaf or bud at the outside turning point of each corner. Yellowwood does not have terminal buds at the ends of its twigs. The last leaf along the twig often looks like an extension of the twig. When a leaf is present on a turning point of the twig, it hides the lateral bud inside the hollow base of its stalk. After the leaves drop for the winter, the remaining fuzzy bud clusters have a horseshoe-shaped leaf scar wrapping around three sides.

Alternately compound leaves (page 104) are 8 to 12 inches (203.2 to 304.8 mm) long with fat arrowhead leaflets, each of which is 2¼ to 4 inches (57.2 to 101.6 mm) long and 1 to 2 inches (25.4 to 50.8 mm) wide. Leaflets are dark green above and lighter beneath, with smooth edges. Yellowwood does not flower every year, but when it does, the white flowers hang in showy clusters. Fruit is a long, flat, curled bean that often hangs on the tree throughout most of the winter.

Features: Yellowwood is a rare tree in nature, but it is getting more and more common in the urban landscape as it is discovered and planted as a feature tree. Pioneers boiled the roots to extract a yellow dye.

Natural Range: The natural range of Yellowwood is limited to populations in southeastern Virginia, western North Carolina and Georgia, west through Tennessee and Kentucky to Arkansas, but it is now more widespread because of urban planting.

The author drew all the illustrations and, with the exception of those credited below, took all of the photographs used in this book.

Wayne Clatterbuck: Bur Oak bark.

Lynden Gerdes @ USDA-NRCS PLANTS Database: Balsam Poplar leaf.

D. E. Herman @ USDA-NRCS PLANTS Database: Black Ash leaf, Black Ash tree, Jack Pine needles, Jack Pine tree, Jack Pine tree row, Jack Pine needles, Ohio Buckeye leaf and fruit, Paper Birch bark, Paper Birch leaf, Paper Birch tree, White Spruce needles, White Spruce tree, White Willow bark, White Willow leaf, White Willow tree.

Carl Hunter @ USDA-NRCS PLANTS Database: Nutmeg Hickory leaf.

Steve Hurst @ USDA-NRCS PLANTS Database: Black Oak acorn, Chestnut Oak acorn, Laurel Oak acorn, Live Oak acorn, Northern Red Oak acorn, Overcup acorn, Pin Oak acorn, Scarlet Oak acorn, Shingle Oak acorn, Shumard Oak acorn, Southern Red Oak acorn, Water Oak acorn, Willow Oak acorn.

Robert H. Mohlenbrook @ USDA-NRCS PLANTS Database: Black Ash bark, Gray Birch Leaf, Poison Oak Leaf, Poison Sumac, Pussy Willow leaf.

Tom Simpson: Pignut Hickory bark, Pignut Hickory tree.

Mark Skinner @ USDA-NRCS PLANTS Database: Carolina Ash leaf.

Clint Strohmeier: Overcup Oak tree, Overcup Oak bark, American Smoke Tree tree, American Smoke Tree bark.

Nathan Waters: Box Elder Tree (summer), Honeylocust thorns, Shortleaf Pine bark resin pockets, Sourwood Bark, Sourwood Tree, Sugar Maple bark.

P. J. Webb: Southern Shagbark Hickory tree.

Index